M Winsor

History of Jewell County, Kansas

with a Full Account of its Early Settlements and the Indian Atrocities

Committed Within its Borders

M Winsor

History of Jewell County, Kansas
with a Full Account of its Early Settlements and the Indian Atrocities Committed Within its Borders

ISBN/EAN: 9783337143817

Printed in Europe, USA, Canada, Australia, Japan

Cover: Foto ©ninafisch / pixelio.de

More available books at **www.hansebooks.com**

HISTORY

- OF -

JEWELL COUNTY, KANSAS.

WITH A FULL ACCOUNT OF ITS

EARLY SETTLEMENTS,

- AND THE -

INDIAN ATROCITIES

Committed Within its Borders.

- o -

Its Final Settlement, Organization and Progress. Its Present
Society, Churches and Schools. Its Towns, Streams,
Topography, Soil and Products. Its Population,
Township Organizations and Officers. Its
Industries, Business, Resources, &c.

- BY -

M. WINSOR and JAMES A. SCARBROUGH.

- o -

JEWELL CITY, KANSAS.
"DIAMOND" PRINTING OFFICE.
1878.

ESTABLISHED JUNE 4, 1871.

Oldest House in Jewell County.

JOHN D. ROBERTSON,

—DEALER IN—   1527691

GENERAL MERCHANDISE,

Farm Implements, Wagons, Cattle, Hogs and Grain.

JEWELL CITY, - - - - - KANSAS.

1872 G. B. CRANDALL, 1878

DRUGGIST AND APOTHECARY.

Jewell City, Kans.

CARRIES A STOCK OF DRUGS COMPLETE IN EVERY DEPARTMENT OF THE BUSINESS.

I give my customers the advantage of any decline in prices and will at all times dispense

Pure Goods,

and guarantee everything as represented.

I also handle

School Books, Blank Books

and kindred goods.

ANY BOOK PUBLISHED IN THE UNITED STATES OBTAINED ON SHORT NOTICE.

INTRODUCTION.

—o—

A complete history of any county is one of the impossibilities, but in this little book, we flatter ourselves that we have come as near perfection as is possible. In the preparation of a work of this kind, we are not unmindful of the fact that in gathering information from so many different sources, inaccuracies are liable to creep in, but in this instance, we have carefully weighed and proved each item, rejecting what seemed to be chaff, and admitting only the bare unvarnished facts. Of the incidents relating to the early history of Jewell county we have only given place to a few of the most interesting, rejecting, of necessity, many that have come into our possession, for want of space. The early history of this county is most intensely thrilling, not a stream or section within its borders but what bears record of the fierce and bloody strife waged by barbarism to beat back the ever advancing tide of civilization.

Citizens of Jewell county, this little work is your friend and co-laborer. In its production, the authors have recognized and acted upon the theory that every dweller on our lovely prairies, and by our timber-belted streams, are, while laboring to plant their own homes in the sunshine of prosperity, also laboring to advance the material interests of the county at large. In this spirit has this work been conceived, nourished, brought forth, and finally offered to you to be a friend and companion at your firesides, and a messenger of good, by disseminating a better knowledge of the county we all think is the best.

Buy one, take it home and read it to your family, and then come back and buy five more copies to send to your friends "Back East." In this way you can help us make a fortune, and very materially assist in building up and enriching one of the fairest counties in all the great New West.

M. WINSOR,

JAMES A. SCARBROUGH.

JEWELL CITY, KANSAS, April, 1878.

JEWELL COUNTY.

JEWELL COUNTY, Kansas, is located in the Northern Tier of Counties, immediately south of the Fortieth Parallel, and west of the Sixth Principal Meridian. It is 150 miles, on an air line, west of the Missouri river. It is 30 miles square, and is divided into 25 Congressional Townships, and contains 576,000 acres of the finest land in all the "Great New West."

STREAMS AND TIMBER.

The principal streams are White Rock, Limestone, Buffalo, Marsh and Brown's creeks. White Rock flows through the second tier of townships, from west to east, emptying into the Republican river 4 miles east of the county line. It has numerous tributaries, both from the north and south, which drain almost the entire northern half of the county, the principal of which are Burr Oak, Walnut and Montana from the north, and Porcupine, Troublesome, Big Timber and John's from the south. Limestone has five principal branches, all flowing in a southerly course, and drains the southwestern part of the county, falling into the Solomon river 5½ miles south of the county line. Buffalo has three principal branches, all of which rise near the centre of the county and flow in a southerly course, forming a junction 6½ miles from the south line of the county; thence running east through the northern portions of the southern tier of townships and emptying into the Republican river 12 miles east of the eastern line of the county. Little Cheyenne is also a tributary of the Buffalo, coming in from the south. Marsh creek has three principal branches, which rise in and drain the eastern middle portion of the county. Brown's creek drains the middle southern portion, emptying into the Solomon river 6½ miles south of the southern line. All of these streams have numerous small tributaries, all of which, with the main streams, are belted with from 10 to 80 rods of timber, consisting of burr oak, ash, hackberry, walnut, red and white elm, box elder, red cedar and cottonwood. It will thus be seen that the county is unusually well watered and timbered.

THE SURFACE

of the county is generally a level and undulating prairie, a narrow line of bluffs running from northeast to southwest, comprising the only rough portion of this "Jewel."

THE SOIL

is a rich, black, vegetable mold, from three to twenty feet deep, all underlaid with porous clay. This country giving unmistakable evidence of having once been the bed of a shallow, warm ocean, with low islands, numerous fossils of tropical vegetation and saurian reptiles having been found.

THE BEST OF WATER

is found everywhere by digging to a depth of from 15 to 60 feet. Fine flowing springs are also numerous.

BUILDING STONE,

of excellent quality, is found in great abundance along the banks of all the streams, many kinds of which can be cut into any desirable shape with a common saw.

POPULATION.

For an inland county, deprived of the help of railroads, the increase in population in Jewell county since 1870, the date of its first permanent settlement, has been most wonderful. In 1870, the population was 205; in 1875, it had increased to 7,651; and in 1877, the official reports place the population at 9,767. Since the last numeration, just one year ago, the immigration to the county has been unprecedented, and we are convinced that we are safe in placing its present population at 12,000. According to official returns, Jewell county has 3,662 school children, which, reckoning 3½ persons to each scholar, which is the customary rule, would make our present population 12,817, an increase of 12,612 in seven years. We challenge any other county in the State, with or without railroads, to produce as favorable a showing.

The Assessors' returns for 1877 show 77,635 acres of land in cultivation in Jewell county.

FIRST SETTLEMENT.

"TOO MUCH INDIAN."

In the spring of 1862 William Harshberger and wife, John Furrows and Asburry Clark, wife and child, from Knox county, Ill., settled on White Rock creek; the first two in Jewell county and the latter just in the west edge of Republic county. Harshberger took the claim now owned by Al. Woodruff, adjoining the town of White Rock. Furrows took one-half of what is now William Nixon's farm, and one-half of the farm now owned by Mrs. Frazier, adjoining Harshberger on the west. All built cabins, broke ground and made preparations for making this beautiful valley their future home. But two incidents in connection with this "first settlement" had the effect to cause them to change their minds and seek a land where their associations were more congenial. These incidents are briefly related as follows:

One day, after having built their cabins, and while resting in fancied security, Mrs. Clark went to visit her sister, Mrs. Harshberger, leaving her little five year old boy at home with his father. During her absence a band of "noble red men," arrayed in all the paraphernalia of savage life, suddenly made their appearance at Clark's cabin. This unexpected and wholly unlooked for "call" so completely embarrassed (?) Clark that, feeling his utter inability to appear to advantage in such august company, he very abruptly and unceremoniously excused himself, and beat a hasty retreat, leaving his almost infant son to do the hospitalities of the mansion alone.

It must be remembered that this little incident occurred two years prior to the great Indian outbreak, which afterwards drenched this fair land in innocent blood and caused the death of so many of our brave and hardy pioneers, and when all the Indians of the Plains were at peace and friendly with the white settlers. Therefore when a settler, living a few miles down the creek, and who was better acquainted with the nature of the "call," came up and found the Indians there, he was not at all alarmed, but on entering the cabin he was not a little surprised to find Clark absent and his innocent little son doing the honors of the shanty, and showing his red visitors everything it contained, much to their amusement. The Indians left shortly afterwards without doing any mischief, but it is an admitted fact that their visit, however friendly, was not appreciated by the Clark family, as they extended no invitation to "call again."

DESPERATE INDIAN BATTLE.

The second incident was a desperate Indian battle between the Sioux and Pawnees near this settlement but a short time subsequent to the incident above narrated, in which the former were victorious. A Pawnee, pursued by two relentless Sioux, sought shelter in Clark's cabin and begged to be hid. Clark refused, telling him that he dared not comply with his request for fear of his own life. His pursuers coming up almost immediately, were about to tomahawk their defenseless victim in the cabin, when Clark interferred, telling them not to kill him there, but to take him away, which they did, taking him a short distance from the cabin and literally cutting him all to pieces. On this visit the Indians told the settlers that they had better leave, as a big war was about to break out, and when it did, the White Rock Valley would not be a very desirable locality in which to reside. By this time it may be imagined that the settlers were getting into a proper frame of mind to take that kind of advice, believing, as they doubtless did, that the country was too new for them to remain. They left.

This was the first ripple of the everflowing tide of civilization that unceasingly moves westward, flooding and subduing nature's wildness. Though it receded, it was soon followed by another, more strong, which in turn, was succeeded by a third, and a fourth, and finally, in 1870, the great tidal wave came along and swept the last vestage of savage power a hundred or more miles farther west.

Second Settlement.

Broken up by Indian Atrocities.— Several Settlers Killed and One Woman Carried into Captivity.

The second settlement of Jewell County was made in the spring of 1866 by William Belknap; John Rice, wife and two children; Nicholas Ward, wife and adopted son; an old man by the name of Flint; Mrs. Sutzer and son; Al. Dart; Arch Bump; Erastus Bartlett, and John Marling, wife and child, who all took claims on White Rock creek. Belknap's claim was five miles west of the present town of White Rock; Marling took a claim near the present town of Rubens; Ward took a claim one mile and a half east of Rubens, now owned by Peter Kearns. Rice and all the others took claims in the immediate vicinity of Ward's, and all of them went industriously to work, improving their new homes, with no fears of danger or molestation. But a change soon came over the spirit of their dreams, which culminated in one of the most

TERRIBLE INDIAN OUTRAGES,

that ever took place on our western frontier. One evening in August of the same year, (1866,) a war party of Cheyennes, numbering about 40, came dashing up to Marling's cabin. When Marling saw them coming, he ran out to where his horses were lariated for the purpose of getting one of them to ride down the creek and give the alarm. Immediately after he left the Indian fiends entered the cabin and placing a rope around Mrs. Marling's neck, they dragged her a short distance into the timber, where the whole party outraged her in the most brutal and fiendish manner, and left her in an insensible condition. Marling fled for assistance to the stockade, just below White Rock City. Thomas Lovewell, an old settler of Republic county; Rice and Bump early the next morning accompanied Marling back up the creek, and when about four miles west of the county line, and about six miles east of the scene of the outrage, they discovered Mrs. Marling roaming about in a dazed condition. Her late terrible sufferings had rendered her perfectly wild, and when she discovered the relief party, she could only see in them her late fiendish and inhuman persecutors, and in order to escape being retaken she continually darted from place to place as fast as her little child, who accompanied her, would permit. It was with considerable difficulty that her husband could get near enough to make her hear her name—"Elizabeth"—called. Hearing her name called, she knew they were friends, and stopped. In the mean time, the Indians had taken all the provisions, and everything in the way of cloth about the cabin, even emptying the feather beds for the ticks, and setting fire to the cabin, had taken their departure.

FALLING BACK.

The entire settlement then took the alarm and fell back to the stockade in Republic county, where they remained for two days, when they all went down to Clyde, in Cloud county, in consequence of a reported general Indian massacre, which, however, proved unfounded. In about five days Mr. Lovewell and his wife returned to their claim, and on the sixth day Ward came back and killed a load of buffalo meat, which he took back to the settlements around Clyde for sale.

RETURNING TO THEIR CLAIMS.

Directly afterwards Lovewell and his wife started out on a buffalo hunt, and found Rice and Bartlett on their claims, to which they had returned by another route. The scare being over the settlers all returned to their claims during the fall, where they remained undisturbed until the next spring, when a second dash upon this unfortunate settlement by the

INHUMAN RED DEVILS

cost the lives of four settlers and drove the rest from the county forever.

On the 9th day of April, 1867, the Cheyennes made another descent upon this devoted settlement, killing Bartlett, Mrs. Sutzer, her little son, and Nicholas Ward, and desperately wounding Ward's adopted son, leaving him for dead, and carrying Mrs. Ward off, a captive. The particulars of this

HORRIBLE MASSACRE

are as follows: The Indians came to Mrs. Sutzer's cabin, where Bartlett was boarding, and demanded dinner, which she proceeded to prepare, in the mean time sending her little son across the creek to Ward's to inform them of the presence of the Indians. Bartlett was down in the timber, splitting rails, and returning for dinner, was met by the Indians and tomahawked as he was passing around the corner of the house. He was found lying on his back, his iron wedge near his right hand and his own knife—a dirk—sticking in his throat. It is thought that when Bartlett was killed Mrs. Sutzer started to run. She was found dead about thirty yards from the house with her skull crushed with a rock. It appears that the cunning fiends had refrained from using firearms for fear of raising an alarm. After completing their bloody work at Mrs. Sutzer's the Indians crossed the creek to Ward's cabin, and again called for dinner, which Mrs. Ward prepared for them. They eat their dinner, smoked their pipes and chatted away in the most friendly manner. At the conclusion of their "smoke," one of them very coolly loaded his gun and asked Ward if he thought it would kill a buffalo. Ward replied that he thought it would. Whereupon the Indian instantly leveled his gun at Ward's breast and shot him through the heart, killing him immediately. The two boys—Ward's and Mrs. Sutzer's—then started to run. The Indians pursued them, following them to the bank of the creek, and shooting them down in the bed of the stream. The Sutzer boy was shot through the heart; instantly killed. The Ward boy was shot through the neck and left for dead. Some time during the succeeding night, however, he recovered his senses, and groping his way back to the cabin in the dark, found the door broken down and entered. Feeling around in the dark with his hands he stumbled and fell over the dead body of his adopted father. Procur-

ing some blankets from one of the beds, he returned to the timber, where he remained the balance of the night, and was found the next morning by a party of claim hunters, to whom he told the above sad and harrowing tale.

It appears that when the Indians ran out to shoot the boys, Mrs. Ward must have shut and bolted the door, when the Indians returning, broke it down and took her prisoner.

HER SAD FATE

will probably never be known, as up to the present time, after the lapse of eleven years, nothing definite has ever been heard of her. Every effort to find her, by Mr. Flint, her grandfather, and by her relatives in Southern Illinois, was made, that love or money could devise, but all to no purpose. She was never found. About two months after her capture an article appeared in the Junction City *Union* which probably throws a little ray of light on this dark page. It was a description of a white woman seen by some negro soldiers, wandering solitary and alone on the Saline river. At their approach she ran out of an old, deserted cabin, and made for the timber, apparently in great terror, evidently mistaking the negro soldiers for Indians. The soldiers, on the other hand, fearing she might be an Indian decoy, did not follow. As their description corresponds with that given of Mrs. Ward, and as nothing has ever since been heard of her, there is but little doubt that it was her, and that she had escaped from the Indians, only to perish of hunger and terror, alone on the silent prairie. Mrs. Ward is described as a tall and prepossessing young woman, not over twenty-two years of age, respectably connected and beloved by all who had the pleasure of her acquaintance.

OUR INDIAN POLICY.

The uncertain fate of Mrs. Ward; the fact that the Government never made any effort to rescue her, or ascertain anything concerning her; the fact that the Indians were all supplied with the most approved arms and ammunition; the fact that the frontier settlers were left wholly unprotected; all, together with a thousand other facts of similar import, go to make up a sad commentary on our Indian policy, as it was, as it is, and as it always will be, until the "Government" learns that it is as much its duty to give full and ample protection to its own citizens as to its murderous, lazy, thieving and treacherous "wards."

THE SURVIVORS.

Mr. Flint was gone to Clyde after a stove for Mrs. Ward at the time of the massacre, and thus escaped the sad fate of his friends. He afterwards returned to Illinois, where he was appointed administrator of a large estate that poor Mrs. Ward had fallen heir to. He never returned to Kansas. His claim was the one now owned by Jno. H. Wadley, one mile east of Rubens. Bartlett's and Bump's claims are now owned by Martin Dahl. Rice's claim is now owned by Peter Tanner.

Marling got his feet frozen in March before the massacre, and with his wife and child, had gone to Missouri. He now lives near Fort Scott, Kansas, and talks of soon returning to Jewell county.

Arch. Bump was waylaid, shot and instantly killed on Upton creek, Cloud county, five miles west of Clyde, in May. Vincent Davis was also shot at the same time, and severely wounded, dying several years afterwards, from the wound. The shooting was supposed to have been done by a couple of Jew peddlers. At least the evidence was so strong against them that they were hung to a tree on Elm creek, in Cloud county.

Al. Dart was absent after a load of provisions. Mrs. Dart returned to Clyde, where she met her husband. Coming to the conclusion that White Rock was not a very healthy locality in which to reside, just at that time, Dart took a claim south of the Republican river, near Clyde, where he has lived ever since, until a few weeks ago, when he died. Mrs. Dart still lives on the Cloud county Homestead.

Rice left, but came back in 1868 on a buffalo hunt, with a company of "tender feet"—new comers—and went into camp one night, four miles up Burr Oak creek. Had their horses stolen b. ..   .. ..l a man in Re-

public county to haul their wagons back to the settlements. Rice never came back. "Too much Indian."

The greatest desire of the Indians, in the matter of plunder, appeared to be cotton cloth, and to that end beds, flour sacks, and even small sacks containing seeds, were emptied of their contents and carried off. The horses and mules of the settlers were taken, but the cattle were left unmolested.

HUNTING INCIDENT,
IN WHICH INDIANS FIGURE.

Before the bloody event narrated in the last chapter, game of all kinds, being plenty, frequent hunting expeditions took place, one of which is related as follows:

In October, 1866, a hunting party made up of the settlers on White Rock, and a party of sportsmen from Nemaha county, all under the lead of S. M. Fisher, of Republic county, went up the creek on a hunt. Near the present town of Holmwood they were joined by Thomas Lovewell and Chauncey Dart, who had also started out on a hunt, and all went into camp together for the night. The next day the whole party went southwest to the Limestone, where Lovewell and Dart separated from the Fisher party, the former going southwest, and the latter going southeast. Soon after their separation, and when only about two miles apart, Fisher's party were suddenly surrounded by a band of about 80 Indians, and offering no resistance, the Indians completely stripped them of all their surplus provisions; revolvers and revolver ammunition, but very humanely allowed them to retain their guns and gun ammunition, and told them they must not hunt there. The whole proceeding was in plain view, and was witnessed by Lovewell and his companion. The Fisher party gladly took the Indians' advice and retraced their steps, camping at night on the same spot where they had camped the previous night. In the morning, a single Indian rode into camp. He took a strong liking to a large powder horn owned by Marling, and was coolly proceeding to appropriate it, when Marling objected and hurled the Indian from him. Then Fisher spoke and said: "Let the d——d red cuss have it, but if ever they come down the creek, we'll give them h——ll." Marling took off the horn and gracefully presented it to the Indian, who put it over his shoulder, mounted his pony, turned suddenly and shot Fisher in the back with his revolver. Fisher carries the ball to this day under his shoulder blade. Marling caught up a Henry rifle and was about to dispatch Mr. Lo, when Fisher interposed, saying: "For God's sake, don't shoot him, for if you do, we will all be killed," and the Indian was allowed to depart in peace. Without doubt a large band of Indians was within hailing distance, and Mr. Fisher did for the best, thus averting another bloody massacre.

"WHITE INDIANS."

Lovewell and Dart, after leaving the other party, went across Oak Creek and finding no game finally reached the Republican river in Nebraska, where they killed a load of elk. Here Al. Dart was also hunting, and seeing Lovewell, took him for an Indian. Running into the timber for his team of cattle, he drove into the settlement in Jowell county that day and night, a distance of fifty miles. When Lovewell got back, three days after, the whole settlement was in a fever of excitement, and preparing to leave, but were persuaded to remain, which they did, until after the massacre in April following, (heretofore described) when the survivors all left, thoroughly disheartened. Thus ended the "Second Settlement" of Jewell County.

Third Settlement,

And Some Incidents Connected Therewith.—Another Victim to Savage Hate.

After the bloody incidents recorded in the preceding chapter, which culminated in the breaking up of the settlement, the Indians were left in undisputed possession of the county for about one year.

February 20, 1868, Richard Stanfield homesteaded the sw¼ Section 9, Township 2 south, Range 6 west. Commuted June 30, 1869. March 18, 1868, Carl G. Smith homesteaded the s½ ne¼ and w½ se¼ Section 7, Township 2 south, Range 6 west. Commuted July 16, 1870. June 26, 1868, Allen D. Woodruff homesteaded s½ se¼ Section 12, and n½ ne¼ Section 13, Township 2 south, Range 6 west. This is the same claim that William Harshberger settled on in 1862, being the first claim taken in the county.

In the spring of 1868, Gordon Winbigler and Adam Rosenberg took claims on White Rock creek, the former taking the claim now owned by Thomas E. West, near Rubens, and the latter taking a claim a short distance west of Rubens. Winbigler was

KILLED BY AN INDIAN

on the 12th day of the following August, on the east side of the Republican river, opposite the mouth of White Rock creek, whither all the settlers in that section of country had congregated for the purpose of fortifying a camp, and preparing for winter. A number of men were out cutting hay, when they were suddenly attacked by a body of mounted Indians. All ran for the camp and escaped except Winbigler, who stopped to pick up his hat which fell off on the way. His anxiety to save his head gear cost him his life, for in stopping to pick up his hat, he was overtaken by an Indian, and was killed by a thrust of his lance, which struck him in the neck, severing the jugular vein. This took place in plain view of all assembled at the camp, including quite a number of women and children.

INDIAN SUPERSTITION.

Winbigler had a little dog, that, after the death of its master, set up a terrible howl. Now the Indians have a superstition that the spirits of those who are killed take the form of animals, and when this little dog set up its mournful howl, they, after several ineffectual attempts to kill it, came to the conclusion that it was Winbigler's spirit, and was there to torment them for his death; to escape which the entire band suddenly withdrew, leaving this whole section free of their presence. This attack on the White Rock settlers was made on the same day that White was killed and his daughter taken prisoner on Granite creek in Cloud county. On this day the Indians made a simultaneous attack on all the settlers along the frontier, from the Saline to the Republican river, murdering about forty men, women and children, indiscriminately.

Adam Rosenberg is still living in the county, though in 1869 he enlisted at Manhattan, in the 19th Kansas Volunteers, and was with Gen. Custer on his famous expedition to the Canadian river, in the Indian Territory, where Mrs. Morgan and Miss White were rescued from the Indians. As his name would imply, Adam Rosenberg is a Dutchman, and is something of an odd genius, commonly called "Old Adam." Adam was present at the death of Winbigler, and afterwards got his hat, and it is thought, got an Indian about the same time, he having fired several shots at them, one appearing to have taken effect. After the killing of Winbigler, Thomas Lovewell and Adam were the only two settlers who remained on the creek that winter, from its head to its mouth, and they employed their time in numerous

HUNTING EXPEDITIONS,

some of which we will briefly notice, on account of the part taken in them by the Indians. In September, 1868, one of these hunts was taken on the Republican river, near the present town of Superior, Nebraska. They were accompanied by James Reed, his son and Robert Watson, from Lake Sibley, in Cloud county. They had just killed their first buffalo, when they discovered a band of 35 Indians making directly for them. The team was sent down a ravine out of sight, while Lovewell and Reed went in another direction to mislead the Indians. This ruse was successful. After getting the Indians far enough

away to insure the safety of the team, they suddenly disappeared down a ravine, and after several miles of pretty fast traveling, again rejoined their friends with the wagon. The last seen of the Indians, they were on the north side of White Rock, near the mouth of John's creek, which was in the direction that Lovewell and Reed first started.

The next day they tried hunting in another direction, going southwest to the forks of Marsh creek. Here the team was left in the thick timber, while Lovewell and Reed started for a herd of buffalo, which could be seen about five miles distant, Adam and the rest of the party remaining on guard near the team. After the hunters had proceeded a part of the way in the direction of the supposed game, they discovered, that instead of buffalo, they were after a party of Indians, who immediately proceeded to hunt them. The hunters took to their heels, and ran about two miles in a southeasterly direction, avoiding the camp, and secreted themselves in the tall grass. The Indians hunted faithfully for them for several hours, sometimes coming rather uncomfortably near them, but failing to find them, withdrew before night. The maneuvers of the Indians were in plain view of the guard left with the team, who supposed that they had killed Lovewell and Reed, and were hunting about for their companions. After dark the hiding hunters returned to camp and rejoined their friends. They remained there all night, and the next morning, having come to the conclusion that there was no chance to kill buffalo, where, as Adam expressed it, they all turned to "Inchins," the party broke up, Adam and Lovewell returning to White Rock, and Reed and his party starting for Lake Sibley, which they finally reached in safety, after again encountering Indians, and being corralled in a ravine for nearly a whole day.

ADAM KILLS AN INDIAN.

A short time after the hunt above noted Lovewell and Adam took one alone. When near the present town of Holmwood Lovewell left the wagon.

for the purpose of killing some buffalo, a herd of which he had seen a short distance off, leaving Adam with team. He had proceeded but a little ways when he discovered three Indians on horseback, riding at a furious speed, directly towards the wagon. He immediately turned and ran to the assistance of his friend. But before coming within gun shot, what was his surprise, without seeing the smoke or hearing the report of a gun, to see one of the Indians suddenly fall from his pony, shot through the heart, the other two Indians only stopping long enough to recover their dead comrade's fire-arms, and then dashing away across the prairie. Lovewell, on coming up to the wagon, said: "Adam, did you see any Indians around here, just now?" Adam replied: "You yoost petter pet I did, sonny." "Did you kill any?" He replied: "I Don't know sonny; I dit my pest; I took goot aim." "Well," said Lovewell, "there's a dead Indian lying up here in the ravine, who tumbled off of his pony a little while ago." This was the first intimation that Adam had that his shot had taken effect, the Indians having passed out of his sight directly after he fired. They then went up to where the dead Indian lay. On approaching him Adam's joy knew no bounds. He fairly danced around his fallen foe with the livliest manifestations of delight. In the wagon were two guns—one a Spencer carbine, that fired eight times, and the other a Star, that only fired once, without re-loading. In his hurry to fire on the Indians Adam had picked up the Star instead of the Spencer. On discovering his mistake Adam was furious with rage, and thus relieved himself: "If I had only not been one tam fool, and had took the Spencer, instead of tat tam Star, I coot haf got two, in place of this tam one."

Lovewell thought it best to leave this vicinity, but Adam insisted on remaining and killing a load of buffalo, remarking: "Who's afraid of two tam Inchins?" Lovewell, however, carried his point, and they returned home, much to Adam's disgust, but it was no doubt for the best.

A FRIENDLY VISIT (?)

On the 12th of July 1868, a large party of Indians came down White Rock and camped near White Rock City. They appeared extremely friendly, and manifested no disposition to harm any one. They were no doubt taking in the "situation" preparatory to the general massacre which took place all along the frontier just one month later, already described. Although they showed no disposition for blood, it was impossible for them to entirely resist their ruling passion—horse stealing. Consequently they picked up all the loose horses that they could lay their hands on, without resorting to violence.

FIGHTING FOR HIS TEAM.

In the month of June 1868, a short time before the "friendly visit" above narrated, two brothers by the name of Catlin, and another man from Manhattan, Kansas, came up to contest the claims of some of those who had been killed in 1867, and took possession of the house in which Mrs. Sutzer and Bartlett were living at the time they were killed. This house stood on the identical spot where Peter Tanner's house now stands, and in which he now lives. The party generally stayed further down the creek, but made occasional trips up to their claims to work. One day George Catlin went with his team up to the cabin after some things. While there a party of "friendly Indians" came up and began to talk "swap." He stood in the door, somewhat dubious, and parleyed with them. Presently one of the Indians commenced to unhitch the team, and Catlin commenced to shoot. The Indians returned the fire, filling the door jamb full of bullet holes. Catlin would shoot and then dodge back out of the way. The Indians finally retired, leaving plenty of blood on the ground, where they had stood, showing the accuracy of Catlin's aim. Catlin was unhurt, but one bullet struck his watch, smashing it all to pieces. These young men, however, concluded not to farm in Jewell county, and packing up their "traps," they changed their place of residence without delay.

Six Hunters Killed.

No One Left to Tell the Sad Story of Their Tragic End.

About the middle of May, 1868, a party of buffalo hunters, six in number, named Lewis Castle, Walter Haines and two Roberts brothers, of Clifton, Kansas, and two brothers by the name of Collins, from near Lake Sibley, Cloud county, Kansas, went on a hunting expedition in the southern part of Jewell county. As they did not return within the expected time, their friends becoming solicitous of their fate, organized a party to go in search of them. The searching party, after two days' hunt, finally struck their trail and followed it to its fatal end, where their sad fate was only too vividly and horrifyingly apparent. There, in a heap, in the bed of the Little Cheyenne, lay their putrefying bodies, a most melancholy and sickening sight to behold. The trail leading to this "Valley of Death" was still painfully visible and, though silent, was a true witness to the particulars of this horrible Indian butchery. The first four hunters named had a horse team and were hunting on Brown's creek, four miles west of where Jewell City now stands. When attacked, they started east, and after going about two miles, were joined by the Collins boys, who had an ox team, which the Indians killed near where the two trails came together. The running fight was continued east to near the crossing of West Buffalo, where the Indians supposing the hunters would cross, had laid an ambush. The hunters, evidently becoming aware of this, suddenly changed their course due south, thereby gaining ground and safely crossing Dry creek, one mile and a half south, and reaching the divide south of Buffalo creek. Here their trail again turned east, giving every evidence, along its entire course, of a desperate conflict. One of the hunters had evidently been shot before reaching the fatal crossing on Little Cheyenne, and had been carried along in the wagon. When found, the bodies were so far decayed and emitted such a sickening odor that the most that could be done for the dead was to throw a few shovelfulls of dirt and lay some stones over them, until the following spring, when their bones were carefully gathered up and properly interred. Whether any Indians were killed will never be known. Thomas Lovewell, wife, and Dan Davis, (Mrs. Lovewell's brother) and wife were camped, on the day this occurred, three miles northwest of Jewell City, on what is now Oliver Smith's farm, also on a hunting expedition, and distinctly heard the sound of voices calling, probably the first party calling the Collins brothers to apprise them of danger.

AN INSCRIPTION.

A FEW WORDS THAT TELL A WHOLE STORY.

In connection with the foregoing tragedy, there is evidence that leaves little or no doubt but that on the same day, a still greater scene of blood was enacted. While searching for the missing hunters, an inscription in pencil was found on a small black walnut tree on Buffalo creek, just above the mouth of Dry creek, which read as follows:

"Had a fight with Indians; 6 of us killed, and 4 taken prisoners."

The tree had been blazed in order to receive the inscription, and attract attention, and if not a most wicked and foolish device to deceive, it told a sad tale in a few words. Now for the corroborating circumstances. On the day previous to the killing of the hunters, a party of six young men, in a spring wagon, crossed the Republican river just above the mouth of Buffalo creek, at the same time the Lovewell party crossed. These young men were from the East, and were in gay spirits, and appeared quite contented with their own company. After crossing the river, these two parties took slightly different courses, Lovewell bearing farther north than the others, but keeping them in view until nearly dark. About 4 P. M. another wagon was seen to join the spring wagon party. Nothing was ever seen or heard of these two wagons, or the men who were with them, except that the irons of a spring wagon were afterwards found near the forks of the Buffalo. If the second wagon contained four men, making ten, the number named in the inscription, four of whom were taken alive, it is reasonable to suppose the prisoners were taken west to the Indian villages in their own wagon, and there suffered death, probably at the stake. Another link in this chain of evidence, is the fact that, several years after this time, the frame of a violin was found near the bluffs, west of Jewell City, where it had apparently lain for years. How came this violin there? It must have been either dropped in flight by the whites, or thrown away as useless, by an Indian, after he had taken it from the whites. What more natural than that this gay party, who seemed bent on having a good time, should have had a violin along to while away the hours? In all human probability, the soil of Jewell county drank on this day, the blood of twelve white men, four more being reserved for torture.

Fourth Settlement.

Another Innocent Life Sacrificed to the Savage Moloch.—"The Excelsior Colony."— Hunters Attacked.—A Gallant Resistance, With Another Bloody Sequel.—Indian Troubles all Along the Line.

Late in October, 1868, a large colony of Scandinavians located on the Republican river, and laid out the town of Scandia, in Republic county, which was the headquarters of the colony. This settlement reached far up the river, and also up White Rock creek, into Jewell county. Several members of this colony contested claims that had been previously taken by parties heretofore mentioned. At this time there was a lively rivalry for these claims, and a number were homesteaded by Swedes, who lived in Junction City, and who would be first notified of their cancellation through the medium of a Swede clerk in the Land Office. Some of the Swedes who took claims at this time, continue to hold them, though none remained permanently in the county until the spring of 1870, and by far the largest number entirely deserted them. The names of those who took land this year, and held it, besides those heretofore mentioned, are Martin Dahl, G. R. Nelson, John Johnson and Peter Tanner. John Dahl settled with the rest, but was killed by Indians in the following spring, an account of which will follow.

In May, 1869, what was known as the "Excelsior," or New York Colony, under the lead of one Walker, came into the county and took claims along White Rock creek, as high up as Burr Oak, and as far down as John's creek. About 3 miles east of the present site of Holmwood, a block house was erected for protection, and surrounded by two lines of earth-works. Here the whole colony resided during its short stay in the county. Immediately after their arrival, they gave public notice that all claimants of land on the creek must be on their claims by a certain date, or they would be contested. This had the effect to bring to the creek a number of Swedes and Norwegians, who laid claim to nearly all the most valuable land. At this time, the latter part of May, 1869, there were over 100 people in the county, all on White Rock creek.

THE BEGINNING OF TROUBLE.

On the 30th day of May, three men came to White Rock and stated that they had started on a hunt from Rose creek, Neb., with a party of seven, but had been attacked by Indians and four of their number killed, and they asked for help to go back and bury their dead companions and recover their wagons. A force of 30 men were raised, and under the lead of Lovewell, proceeded to the scene of the massacre, which occurred partly in the Northwest corner of Jewell county, and partly on the Republican river in Nebraska, where the wagons were found, and two of the dead men, with every evidence of a desperate resistance. The two dead men at the wagons were buried, but the others were not found for some time after. They had fallen in this county, adding the blood of two more victims to its soil. During the return of the burial party, Indians were visible at a distance, they judging the whites too strong to be safely attacked. On the 23d, they got back as far as the "Excelsior Colony" fortifications, and on the morning of the 24th, those who did not belong to this colony, proceeded down the creek, dropping out as fast as they came to their claims. Upon arriving at Peter Tanner's place, that individual came out of the brush and informed them that on the previous day, the Indians had made a raid at this point, and shot Johnny Dahl, and burnt several cabins, destroying a large amount of property, and run off much stock. The smoking ruins of Pete's house attested the truth of his statement. At this moment, a party of horsemen were seen coming, and the little army, now numbering only 16, prepared for battle, but the horsemen proved to be whites, from Salt creek, out after some wagons that had been left hid in Upper Elm Grove, on the Republican river, now McCraken's Grove, while two hunters were run home by Indians. It was afterwards learned that these wagons and teams were found all right, the Indians not happening to go that way. As Lovewell and his party proceeded down the creek, they were continually seeing the heads of men peeping at them over some hill, or from some ravine in the distance, appearing for a moment, then disappearing, only to be seen again at some other point. Finally chase was made, and two of these mysterious persons caught, and the mystery was solved. Nearly the whole Swede settlement had taken flight, and in their fright saw Indians in this band of horsemen. It is not strange they were frightened, all unused as they were to scenes of blood. Johnny Dahl had been carried six miles down the creek, on a door, mortally wounded, and left at Al. Woodruff's house, where he died at 11 o'clock at night, the day previous to Lovewell's return. That night nearly all the Swedes and Norwegians left the creek and went back to Scandia.

SIX MORE HUNTERS KILLED.—ONE ESCAPES TO TELL THE STORY.

On the 26th, only two days subsequent to the attack on the Swede settlement, a party of seven hunters from Irving, Kansas, were attacked just south of Wilson's Grove, on the Republican river, in the north part of the county, and slowly fought their way back to a block house, just in the edge of Republic county, and about 2 miles north of White Rock creek. The firing was distinctly heard on the creek during nearly the whole of the afternoon. This party remained safely at the block house during the night, and in the morning, no enemy being visible, started for home. Upon reaching the Republican river, the Indians again attacked them, and having expended all their amunition in the fight of the previous day, the whole party broke for the water, and six were overtaken and shot in the stream, one only escaping, John McChesney, an uncle of the John W. McChesney, so well known in newspaper circles in Northwestern Kansas.

The firing was distinctly heard on White Rock, and a party would have went to the assistance of the hunters, but were prevented by a big rise in the creek, making a crossing impossible.

MORE MISCHIEF.

On the following day, (the 27th) about 60 Indians swam across the creek, about half a mile east of the county line, and skulking up a ravine, attempted to surprise three Swedes—Munson, Burcham and Hageman—whose claims were in Jewell county, but who were then helping a friend to put in corn just over the line. They had become tired and had sat down to rest, unconcious of danger. Lovewell, who was at work close by, saw the Indians, and ran down to save the Swedes. Arriving within about 60 yards of them, he saw an Indian's head and gun cautiously raised up out of the head of the ravine, evidently bent on mischief. He instantly leveled his rifle at the Indian, who, as suddenly ducked down again. The next instant the 80 savages sprang from their cover in a body, and began to circle, as is their mode. Lovewell held his rifle to his face, first bearing on one and then on another, and slowly backing until the Swedes had reached the other end of the field, where they had left their carbines and revolvers. After this the Indians kept a safer distance for both parties. When he first discovered the Indians, Lovewell ordered Burchlam to secure the horses he was driving. But he was so stupefied that when the other men had secured their weapons, he still stood looking on in a dazed way, not having made a move towards securing the team. He was again ordered to save the team, and striking them with the lines, they became frightened and ran away with the plow. In a few minutes the plow struck something and became detached, and the horses ran and mixed with the circling ponies of the Indians—just what the latter most desired. The raid was made about 3 p. m., and the Indians withdrew about dusk. But two or three shots were fired by the whites, the Indians, after the first rush, keeping at too great a distance. Lovewell, who at first was close enough, wisely held his fire, in strict accordance with the only true tactics in such trying emergences. Had he fired, instead of simply covering the Indians with his rifle, in all human probability not a man of the whole party would have escaped. As it was, the only loss sustained was that of the team. In this place we will add that on the day Johnny Dahl was killed, the Indians took Al. Woodruff's team, leaving him afoot and without the means to buy another.

A PLUCKY WOMAN.

At this time, Mrs. Frazier, a widow woman who now lives in Jewell county, was living on a rented place about a mile east of the county line. While the Indians were skirmishing with Lovewell and the Swedes, a number of them paid her a visit. A man by the name of Robert Watson, was out in the field plowing with a span of horses, and the Indians had entirely cut him off from the house and was about to take him in, when Mrs. Frazier ran out with a double-barreled shot gun and fired several shots at them, and drove them back until Watson gained time to unhitch, and come in with the horses. The Indians gave her no further trouble, and soon took their departure.

BUCKSKIN TAKES A BATH.

Just as the Indians crossed the creek an Irishman, who went by the name of "Buckskin," and who had come out with Mrs. Frazier, had been up to Lovewell's, and had started home, but had proceeded but a short distance when he discovered the Indians. When he saw them he ran down to the creek, and plunging into the water he got under a large drift, where he remained all night in the water, only venturing out at daylight, nearly chilled to death. The joke was on "Buckskin," for the Indians had not seen him at all.

THE EXCELSIOR COLONY LEAVES.

Mrs. Frazier had two sons—Frank and William—who had been employed to go up to the "Excelsior Colony" and move one of the families out of the country. Contrary to advice the boys started up the creek that morning and arrived safe enough at the colony fort; got the family—husband and wife and their effects into the wagon, making a big load. They were city bred and in fair circumstances, having several trunks of fine clothing, rich dresses and millinery. On their return they had reached John's Creek, when lo! a hundred Indians made their appearance on the bluffs above them. Seeing no chance of escape the Frazier boys cut the horses loose from the wagon, and mounting them started back for the fort, pursued by the Indians. After a short run, seeing that they were about to be overtaken they jumped from their horses and taking to the timber on foot, made their escape. The husband and wife at the the wagon, with two Englishmen who belonged to the Colony, ran down John's Creek, and assisting the woman, crossed the swollen White Rock, and escaped, reaching Lovewell's at 3 a. m., the next morning. In their flight they followed every tortuous bend of the stream, not daring to cross the open spaces for fear of being seen and butchered by the Indians. The woman was a sad sight to look upon when she arrived. Having had to cross the stream several times, in order to facilitate her flight, she had taken off all her clothing but one dress, her peticoats being so heavy with water that she could not walk with them on.

The Indians broke open all the trunks and boxes at the wagon and rigged themselves out in gorgeous array with the contents. As the party appeared at the fort later in the day one old Indian had on a silk dress and a fancy trimmed lady's hat. They gathered on the bluffs about half a mile south of the fort and treated the terrified inmates to some original dramatic attitudes, which, however, it must be admitted, were not appreciated at the time.

The President of the colony, Mr. Walker, being down at Junction City at the time, heard of this raid on his way back, hired a lot of men and teams, came up and took the colony away, leaving about the first of June. It will be remembered that nearly all the Swedes had left only a few days previous, and when the Colony left these few went also, leaving not a white man or woman in Jewell county. From this time, (June 1st, 1869,) the Indians held undisputed possession of Jewell county until August following, but few whites remaining even in Republic county. But among them was Mrs. Frazier, who did not leave for a month or more. She came back with her two sons in 1870 and still remains a permanent resident of the county.

ANOTHER NEW SETTLER.

In August 1869 Peter Kearns ventured into the county and took the Nicholas Ward claim and remained working on it all the following winter, the sole occupant of Je county. However, in December of that year Robert Clellan picked out a claim, but did not settle on it until the spring of 1870. So to Peter Kearns alone belongs the honor of spending the winter of 1869-70 in Jewell county. He has spent several winters since, but with each succeeding winter the number of his fellow citizens has increased until now he can count them by the thousands. The Indians have entirely disappeared, not only from Jewell county, but from the entire State, not a hostile red man being nearer our borders than five hundred miles.

From the preceding pages it would appear that nearly all the blood shed in Jewell county was on the part of the Indians. But such is not the case, in evidence of which we here give an account of a

DESPERATE BATTLE WITH INDIANS.

In the fall of 1861, a desperate battle took place between a scouting party of soldiers and citizens from Fort Kearney, and a band of Indians, at the forks of East Buffalo creek, on the farm now owned by Joseph Collar. Thirty Indians were killed and one white man—John Collins. The remainder of the Indians were taken prisoners. The Indians were buried in two trenches, and Collins was buried in a grave on the bank of the creek, with head and foot stones to mark the spot. This incident was related to us by William R. Whitney, to whom it was told by one of the participants, who now resides at Fairbury, Nebraska.

Final Settlement.

The Great Influx of 1870.—The Permanent Settlement of the County.—Its Organization, First Election and Some Interesting Incidents Connected Therewith.— Also a few More Indian Raids.

Before detailing the great influx of immigration, which came in in 1870, we will go back to 1869, and give a list of the few claims taken that year that were finally proved up on, and the settlers became permanent residents.

May 22, 1869, James A. Highland homesteaded the s ½ ne ¼ and n ½ se ¼ Section 8, Township 6 south, Range 6 west. Proved up April 9, 1876. Still lives in the county.

May 24, 1869, Nels. S. Cederberg homesteaded the s ½ se ¼ Section 5 and n ½ ne ¼ Section 8, Township 2, south, Range 7, west. Commuted July 16, 1870.

May 26, 1869, William D. Street homesteaded the ne¼ Section 8, Township 5 south, Range 7 west. Commuted July 9, 1871. Farm now owned by Hon. Benj. F. Ransford, Chairman Board of County Commissioners.

November 6, 1869, Peter Kearns homesteaded the se¼ Section 2, Township 2 south, Range 7 west. Commuted July 21, 1873.

November 13, 1869, James McCraith homesteaded the sw¼ Section 1, Township 2 south, Range 6 west. Proved up August 16, 1876. McCraith came back in January 1870, and has remained a permanent resident ever since.

THE TIDAL WAVE

of 1870 commenced in February. In that month John O'Roak, William Scott, Samuel Sweet, Wils. McBride, Chris. Erns, John W. McRoberts, Sam. Bowles, T. Bowles, Phil. Baker, Adams and Gregory came in, all taking claims on White Rock. In the same month, A. J. Davis, Jerry Burnett, L. M. Stults, Benjamin Lewis and Charles Lewis came in and settled on Buffalo creek.

TOO NUMEROUS TO MENTION.

From this time, (February, 1870) the settlers came in so thick and fast that we find it impossible to keep track of them with any kind of accuracy. Consequently we are under the necessity in this place of omitting the names of many, and only giving those of a few of the most prominent in each section of the county. The names of the first settlers of each Township will appear in our description of Townships.

THE BUFFALO PIONEERS.

The first permanent settlers of the Buffalo Valley were Henry Sorick, Geo. A. Sorick, John A. Sorick, Geo. W. Waters, R. F. Hudsonpelier, Thomas B. Hart and William Cox, who took claims in the immediate vicinity of Jewell City, April 8, 1870.

The next arrivals were S. R. Worick, John H. Worick, John Hoffer, Joseph W. Fogle, Cyrus Bichart, Chris. Bender, David J. Rockey, William H. Cameron, Samuel Krape, C. A. Belknap and A. J. Wise, known as the "Illinois Colony," who arrived at the forks of Buffalo creek, April 12, 1870. They all took claims in the vicinity of Jewell City, and all, with the exception of Mr. Cameron, remained until "the war was over" and very materially assisted in "holding the creek" during the somewhat troublesome season of 1870.

The next arrivals on this side of the county were James A. Scarbrough and William Queen, who took claims four miles north west of Jewell City, April 24, 1870. Mr. Queen went back to Clyde, where he had left his family and remained until the first of the following October, when he returned, and has lived here ever since. Scarbrough remained with "the boys" and took an active part in the stirring events of the succeeding summer and fall.

During the month of April, 1870, quite a number of other settlers arrived and took claims in the southern part of the county. Prominent among them were Charles L. Seeley, Isaac A. Sawin, Allen Lightner, Wm. M. Jones, James W. Hall, Richard D. Furdy, L. J. Calvin, F. A. May and John R. Wilson. The majority of them remained, and are among our most enterprising and respectable citizens.

BIG INDIAN SCARE.—THREE MEN KILLED AT THE MOUTH OF THE LIMESTONE.

The settlers all went to work with a will, breaking prairie, building cabins, digging "dug outs" and otherwise improving their claims, with scarcely a thought of danger, until the night of May 12, 1870, when they were all aroused from their peaceful slumbers by a couple of couriers from the mouth of the Limestone, who brought the unpleasant news that the noble Cheyennes were

AGAIN ON THE WAR PATH,

I had only the day before killed three white men who were working on a mill dam on the Solomon, the present site of the fine flouring mill at Glen Elder. The couriers advised all the settlers to repair at once to

"Hoffer's shanty," near the forks of Buffalo creek, and take some steps toward an organization for self protection, as in their scattered condition they would fall an easy prey to the blood-thirsty savages, in case they should take a notion to pay them a visit. It is almost needless to say that this advice was taken and acted upon in the promptest manner imaginable.

By daybreak the next morning, (May 13, 1870) 28 settlers had gathered together at the designated place of rendezvous, and to draw it mild, while the excitement was not intense, the cause of their coming together was the all absorbing topic of conversation. After a hasty breakfast, the meeting was called to order by William D. Street, who, in a few brief rema k , explained the object of the same, and strongly urged the immediate organization of a company of militia with regularly elected officers for the protection of the lives and property of the

SCATTERED SETTLERS.

He also recommended the erection of a fort, and a fraternal banding together for the purpose of "holding the creek." He was followed by several others with remarks of similar import, all agreeing that if the Indians were allowed to run riot all over this valley the present season, the settlement, at least of this portion of the county, would perhaps be deferred for years. All had come here with the avowed intention of remaining and securing homes for themselves and "the loved ones to come," and they did not propose to be run out of the country, simply by a little Indian scare, or, at least, until they had had a sample interview with Mr. Lo. The consequence was, a resolution was adopted to the effect that they organize a company, and

BUILD A FORT

at once. On the organization of the company, the following volunteers stepped to the front and placed their names on the roll of the "Buffalo Militia." We give their names in the exact order in which they appear on the original roll, which was a common buff envelope, now in our possession:

L. J. Calvin, F. A. May, W. M. Jones, Samuel Krape, Louis A. Dapron, C. L. Seeley, J. A. Scarbrough, Cyrus Richart, Chris. Bender, J. H. Worick, David J. Rockey, James W. Hall, Richard D. Fardy, Charles J. Lewis, C. A. Belknap, A. J. Wise, John Hoffer, William Cox, S. R. Worick, Allen Lightner, James F. Queen, J. W. Fogel, J. A. Sorick, R. F. Hudsonpeller, I. A. Sawin, Henry Sorick, Wm. D. Street and John R. Wilson.

These names (28 in number), comprised all the settlers on Buffalo creek at that time, west of "Davis' Ranch." On the election of officers, William D. Street was elected Captain; Charles J. Lewis, First Lieutenant; Louis A. Dapron, Second Lieutenant, and James A. Scarbrough, Orderly Sergeant. Having their teams and breaking plows with them, this spartan band at once repaired to the present town site of Jewell City, and commenced the erection of

FORT JEWELL,

by selecting a spot of ground 50 yards square, around which they immediately commenced breaking the sod, cutting it into squares of the desired size, and laying up a wall. In two days their work was complete, showing a good substantial wall, four feet thick and seven feet high. As soon as the fort was completed, the company turned their attention to digging and walling a well in the northwest corner of the inclosure, which was soon finished, affording an abundance of the best of cold water. This was

THE FIRST WELL DUG

in the county that we have any account of. It is 29 feet deep, and is still in good condition. It is now the property of the Jewell City Town Company, being situated in the edge of Delaware street.

MOUNTING GUARD.

The settlers remained in the fort, off and on, until the 28th of June, 1870, mounting guard a part of the time, during the night, and keeping scouts out during the day. During this time, the men would work on their claims in the day time, but at night they generally returned to the fort, feeling a little safer under the protection of its friendly walls than on their claims. However they were never attacked, and the Indians, although often seen in the immediate vicinity of the fort, never gave the settlers any trouble. At this time, (June 28, 1870,) after the Indian scare was all over, Col. Weir, of the 3rd U. S. Mounted Artillery, sent a company of soldiers to our relief, who took up their quarters in the fort, and gallantly remained with and protected us until late in the fall. But as soon as the soldiers came, the settlers deserted the fort almost entirely, only returning occasionally to beg tobacco of each other, and laugh over the funny incidents of the ever memorable 12th and 13th of May.

OUR LIMITED SPACE

forbids as extensive an account of the early settlement of the Buffalo Valley as we would like to give, and those of our friends among the pioneers, who fail to find their names and date of settlement in this little volume, will please attribute the fact to the proper cause.

MORE NEW SETTLERS.

During the months of May and June, our numbers were increased by the arrival of Col. E. Barker, O. L. McClung, W. C. McClung, R. R. McClung, Z. F. Dodge, J. K. Dodge, F. T. Gandy, H. P. Gandy, L. C. Gandy, Gabe. B. Wade, P. R. Deal, Samuel Cameron, C. E. Plowman, Jonathan Street, Geo. F. Lewis, James Carpenter, Jacob S. Jackson, W. R. Phillips, and many others, whose names we have forgotten. The name of Jesse N. Carpenter does not appear in either of the above lists, from the fact that we copy from the old muster roll, and as Mr. Carpenter was not a member of the organization, his name fails to appear. He was a resident of the county, however, from early in the spring of 1870, and still remains, one of our most influential and worthy citizens.

THE FIRST WHITE WOMAN

who became a resident of the southern part of Jewell county, was Mrs. Annie Billings, wife of N. H. Billings, who arrived at Fort Jewell, May 22, 1870. She was accompanied by her little 10

year old sister, Miss Jennie Jones, who is now married and lives on Wolf creek, in Cloud county.

THE SECOND INVOICE

of white women who came to cheer the bachelor pioneers with their refining and moralizing presence were: Mrs. Adaline Serick, Mrs. Jennie Halstead, Mrs. Annie Waters and Mrs. Mariah Dodge, all of whom arrived at Fort Jewell on the evening of July 3, 1870.

THE FOURTH OF JULY.

The Indians having taken their departure to more inviting fields of blood and plunder, and the country being comparatively safe, the pioneers resolved to celebrate the anniversary of the Nation's birth-day on rather a novel plan. To this end, a committee was appointed to build an arbor near the fort; another to go out on the buffalo grounds and kill a load of fresh beef, and still another to barbecue the buffalo meat after it was brought in. Col. E. Barker was appointed President, and W. R. Phillips Orator of the day. The various committees discharged the duties assigned them with fidelity, and when the day dawned, all was in readiness. The ladies of Clyde and Lake Sibley kindly furnished the light bread, pies, cakes, butter and preserves, and many of them favored the occasion with their fair presence. The attendance was good, all the settlers in the southern part of the county being present, with the exception of a small settlement on Brown's creek, consisting of B. G. Williams and wife, Al. Williams, Wesley Harberson and wife, Jacob Presler wife and daughter, James Presler and James Williams. They had settled there only a short time previous, and were unaware of any settlement but their own in the county. Besides the settlers there were very respectable delegations from Clyde, Lake Sibley and Manhattan. Among the latter was our present respected fellow citizen, J. C. Postlethwaite, who acted in the capacity of Chaplain and invoked the Divine favor. The programme was carried out to the letter. Col. Barker presided with his usual dignity, and

Mr. Phillips "soared the eagle." The dinner was all that could be desired. There was an abundance for all, and plenty left. The "Buffalo Militia" fired a National salute, and the "day's doings" closed with three rousing cheers for our country and the Buffalo Pioneers. At night there was a platform dance under the arbor, of the most primitive character, in which nearly the entire company participated.

PIONEER FRIENDSHIP.

We have enjoyed seven recurrences of "the day we celebrate" in Jewell City since that time, in which there was more display, but you can not make one of those old pioneers beleive but what he had a better time at the "Fourth" in 1870 than he has ever had since. We will not shock our eastern readers with the intimation that the absence of the "jerked buffalo meat" from these latter occasions may be the cause of all this. No, it was the associations of the time; the hardships, trials, dangers and privations of these early days, mutually shared together, that causes the heart of the early pioneer to beat with a quicker throb as he grasps with alacrity the hand of one of those old time-tried friends. They love to live those days over again. They never tire of the buffalo hunts they have taken together; of the bivouac by that little creek "over yonder," or on the silent prairie, with nothing but a buffalo robe and the broad, blue canopy of Heaven for a shelter. Their hearts are indelibly intertwined, and no changes of time or place can effect any permanent change in their feelings towards eachother. But we will spare our readers any further elaboration of the subject. Space forbids, and even if we made the attempt, no one would understand it but the old pioneers themselves. Deep down in the secret recesses of their hearts they feel and know how it is, but language is inadequate to the task of expressing it. They are friends in the deepest, broadest, fullest acceptation of the term, and pioneering has made them so. Pioneers, are we correct or not? We know your kind, sympathetic hearts. "Yes!"

JEWELL CITY.

The beautiful town site of Jewell City was selected and filed on under the Town Site Act, May 6, 1870. On Friday, May 28, 1870, the Jewell City Town Company was organized with the following members: Henry Sorick, Geo. A. Sorick, Geo. W. Waters, R. F. Hudsonpeller, William D. Street, James A. Scarbrough, S. R. Worick, Dennis Taylor, and N. H. Billings. The company met at the house of Esquire Collins, near the mouth of Buffalo creek, in Cloud county, on Friday, June 11, 1870, and acknowledged the signing of the charter, which was sent to Col. Thomas Moonlight, Secretary of State, at Topeka, and by him recorded and a certified copy returned to them. The town site comprised the sw ¼ Section 30, Township 4 south, Range 7 west. The south west quarter of the town site was at once surveyed and laid off into town lots, the remainder being left "until further orders." No improvements were made, however, until the 30th day of June 1870, when

THE FIRST BUILDING

was erected by James A. Scarbrough, for an office and store. This was one of the most primitive buildings ever erected in any country. It was 16 feet square and was constructed by setting a lot of posts in the ground and boarding them up with box lumber. The roof was composed of the same material. The building was commenced in the morning, and by the middle of the afternoon was completed. That evening Scarbrough's goods arrived, and

THE FIRST STORE

was opened in Jewell City, being also the first one ever opened in Jewell county. The stock consisted of groceries, provisions, cigars, chewing and smoking tobacco, baking powders and Hostetter's bitters, and invoiced just $130.65. Mrs. Mariah Dodge and David H. Halstead soon after erected a dwelling house each, and Scarbrough soon followed with a more substantial building, known then and now as

THE PIONEER DRUG STORE.

These were the only buildings in the town when the county was organized.

20

THE LAST INDIAN RAID

made in Jewell county, was on the 10th day of May 1870, when a band of Indians, supposed to be Cheyennes, made a descent on Bowles' settlement on White Rock, and stole two spans of horses—one from Sam. C. Bowles and the other from Peter Tanner. Bowles made a gallant fight for his, firing thirteen shots at the Indians, who in turn fired six gun shots and seven arrows at Mr. Bowles. None of the shots, however, took effect, as Sam. escaped with his scalp lock in its accustomed place, and no dead Indians were found lying around loose. They got his team, however, which he never recovered. Peter Tanner was more lucky. Towards night of the same day, while out looking for them, Peter found his horses in a ravine, on the north side of White Rock, where they had been hid by the Indians.

A FUNNY INCIDENT

connected with the Indian visit to Bowles, goes to prove that their object was more for plunder than blood. One old Indian who appeared to be the leader, stepping up close to Mr. Bowles fired his pistol in the direction of Bowles, the shot striking the ground a few feet from him. Bowles is accused of making the remark: "You d——d old scoundrel; give me that pistol, and I'll make a better shot than that." The Indian, however, did not comply with Bowles' request, whereupon Sam made for the house, met his wife who was coming to him with his weapons, and fired the ineffectual shots above noted.

ORGANIZATION OF THE COUNTY.

Early in July a petition was circulated by Col. E. Barker and Orville L. McClung for an organization of the county, which after being numerously signed was presented to Gov. James M. Harvey at Topeka by Col. Barker, who carried the same there in person. The prayer of the petitioners was granted July 14, 1870, on which day C. L. Seeley, F. T. Gandy and A. J. Davis were commissioned County Commissioners of Jewell county; James A. Scarbrough was commissioned County Clerk, and Jewell City

was designated as the county seat. July 20, 1870, Col. Barker returned to Jewell City, and presented the newly appointed officers with their commissions. Col. Barker was commissioned Notary Public of Jewell county on the 16th day of June, 1870, being the first officer, either elected or appointed, in the county.

SWEARING THEM IN.

On the 4th day of August, 1870, the newly appointed county officers called on Col. Barker at his shanty on Middle Buffalo, one mile and a half north of Jewell City, and there and then, standing out in the open air, on the bank of the historic Buffalo, they were duly sworn into office by Col. Elden Barker, the first Notary Public of Jewell county. Returning to town they effected a temporary organization of the Board, and instructed the County Clerk to give public notice of their first formal meeting, which was set for August 22, 1870. In accordance with said notice

THE FIRST MEETING

of the Board of County Commissioners, in and for Jewell county, Kansas, was held at the office of the County Clerk, in Jewell City, on Monday, August 22, 1870. At this meeting, C. L. Seeley was elected Chairman of the Board, and the county was divided into three Commissioners' Districts, of equal size, and five municipal Townships, as follows: Vicksburg, comprising Townships 3, 4 and 5 south, Range 6 west; Buffalo, comprising Townships 3, 4 and 5 south, Ranges 7 and 8 west; Limestone, comprising Townships 3, 4 and 5 south, Ranges 9 and 10 west; White Rock, comprising Townships 1 and 2 south, and Ranges 9 and 10 and west half of Range 8 west, and Big Timber, comprising Townships 1 and 2 south, Ranges 6 and 7, and east half of Range 8 west, with the voting precinct designated in each. At this first meeting, an order was made for an election for the purpose of electing County and Township officers and

LOCATING THE COUNTY SEAT,

to come off on the 27th day of September 1870. Notice of the approaching election was given by written

1

notices posted up in each Township, and came off on the day designated. The result of this first election was as follows:

For County Commissioners: First District, Dennis Taylor; Second District, Thomas Coverdale. Third District, Samuel C. Bowles. For County Clerk, James A. Scarbrough; for County Treasurer, Henry Sorick; for County Surveyor, N. H. Billings; for Register of Deeds, S. O. Carman; for Probate Judge, Charles L. Seeley; for Sheriff, A. J. Davis; for Coroner, William Cox; for County Superintendent. S. E. Worick; for County seat, Jewell City. An imaginary town on the divide between White Rock and the head of East Buffalo, called Springdale, received 24 votes "for the county seat." It is almost useless to add that Springdale never had an existance in this county, and was never heard of after the county seat election of 1870.

THE SECOND ELECTION

in Jewell county was held on Tuesday, November 8, 1870, at which Felix T. Gandy was elected Representative to the State Legislature; John Hoffer, County Commissioner, First District; Thomas Coverdale, County Commissioner Second District; Seth Hong, County Commissioner, Third District, James A. Scarbrough, County Clerk; A. B. Kellogg, County Treasurer; N. H. Billings, County Surveyor; S. O. Carman, Register of Deeds; A. J. Davis, Sheriff; Abraham Jackson, Probate Judge; Thomas R. Comstock, County Superintendent; R. F. Hudsonpeller, County Attorney, and William Cox, Coroner.

TOWNSHIPS.

BUFFALO TOWNSHIP

was organized at the first meeting of the Board of County Commissioners, August 22, 1870, and was composed of Townships 3, 4, and 5, south, Ranges 7 and 8, west.

THE FIRST ELECTION

for Township officers was held on Tuesday, September 27th, 1870, at which David H. Halstead was elected

Justice of the Peace; Jesse N. Carpenter, Township Trustee; Z. F. Dodge, Township Treasurer; Wm. M. Jones, Township Clerk, and John K. Dodge, Constable. Jesse N. Carpenter failed to qualify as Township Trustee, and on February 20th, 1871, Wm. H. Cameron was appointed by the Board of County Commissioners to fill vacancy, and qualified the same day. The first regular election for Township officers in Buffalo Township was held April 3d, 1871, at which the following officers were elected: J. L. Wegeman, Trustee; Z. F. Dodge, Treasurer; Wm. M. Jones, Clerk; Wm. H. Cameron and B. G. Williams, Justices of the Peace, and James Presler and John K. Dodge, Constables.

THE FIRST SETTLERS

of Buffalo Township have already been named among the "Buffalo Pioneers." Hence we omit them here.

Buffalo Township, since its first organization, has been reduced to one Government Township (Township 4, Range 7.) Prairie, Brown's Creek, Calvin, Centre and Washington having been formed out of its original territory. It now contains six miles square of the finest land in the county, all of which is susceptible of the most successful cultivation, and all of which is taken up. It is well watered by Buffalo and Spring creeks, and is thickly settled by as intelligent, energetic, industrious and moral a community as can be found in any country. There are four school districts, in all of which are good substantial school houses, in which regular terms of school are taught. There are six church organizations—Methodists, Evangelicals, Christians, Baptists, Presbyterians and Catholics, all of whom have regular preaching. The Methodists and Evangelicals each have a nice church building, and the Christians and Catholics are preparing to build. There are four Sunday Schools in the Township, all of which are largely attended. The present population of the Township is 613.

THE PRESENT TOWNSHIP OFFICERS,

elected November 6, 1877, are: James A. Scarbrough, Trustee; M. F. Knappenberger, Clerk; R. W. Hill, Treasurer; A. L. Marks and Nicholas Gishwiller, Justices of the Peace, and M. W George and S. B. Scott, Constables.

ALLEN TOWNSHIP

is situated in the extreme southeast corner of Jewell county; it is six miles square and is well watered by Buffalo and Little Cheyenne creeks, on which a liberal supply of good native timber is found. These streams afford good running water all the year round. In addition to the timber, there is a most abundant supply of building stone, of excellent quality, from which good, subtantial houses are built.

THE FIRST SETTLERS

of Allen Township were A. J. Davis, John B. Keyes, M. L. Stults, M. Betzner, Milton Sadler, William Jones, Ed. D. Randall and R. M. Brigham.

Allen Township was organized August 10, 1872, and was named in honor of our present efficient County Clerk. When organized M. L. Stults was appointed Trustee; Geo. W. Clark, Clerk; D. McKellar and —— Rogers Justices of the Peace, and W. Lattimore. Constable. The majority of these officers were elected at the first regular election the next spring.

Taken as a whole, Allen is a fair average township, with regard to the beauty and fertility of its lands; the energy and intelligence of its people; its numerous well cultivated farms and its neat and substantial farm houses, all of which speaks of thrift, happiness and prosperity.

SCHOOLS AND CHURCHES.

There are two good, substantial school houses in the township—one in District No. 23, and the other in District No. 52, in both of which regular terms of school are taught, and religious services held by the Presbyterians and Methodists.

The public land is all taken, with the exception of School land, and all that is sold that is worth buying.

THE PRESENT TOWNSHIP OFFICERS,

elected November 6, 1877, are Jonathan Corn, Trustee; Milton Sadler, Clerk; J. Chitty, Treasurer; P. F. Pierce, and W. P. Phillips, Justices of the Peace, and M. W. Loop and Thomas J. Hutchison, Constables.

BROWN'S CREEK TOWNSHIP

was originally a portion of Buffalo Township. It was organized August 10, 1872.

THE FIRST ELECTION

was held April, 1, 1873, at which Andrew S. Clelland was elected Trustee; John O'Conner, Clerk; B. G. Williams, Treasurer; Judge A. Jackson and Jacob Presler, Justices of the Peace, and A. G. Williams and James Barton, Constables.

THE FIRST SETTLERS

were B. G. Williams and wife; Jacob Presler, wife and daughter; Wesley Harberson and wife; A. G. Williams, James S. Williams. James Presler, William Booth and James Lampson, who all took claims on the 5th day of June, 1870. The first homestead taken in the Township was by A. G. Williams. The first death was that of Benjamin Lyons, which occurred February 22, 1872. The first birth was a boy born to Mr. and Mrs. W. H. Snyder. The first marriage was Estep Munks to Miss Emily Barnett, in October 1872.

SCHOOLS AND CHURCHES.

There are five school districts in the Township, all of which have school houses, in which regular terms of school are taught. The religious denominations are the Christians and Methodists, both of which have regular preaching and Sunday Schools. There is also a Union Sunday School, which was organized March 25, 1877. All of them are well attended, and are in a flourishing condition. The morals of the Township are most excellent; the people are intelligent, industrious and sociable. Consequently they are prosperous and happy.

Brown's Creek Township comprises all of Township 5, south, Range 8, west, and is by far the finest Township of land in the county, there not being a forty acre lot in the whole Township but what can be successfully cultivated. It is watered by Brown's Creek and a small tributary of Buffalo, both of which afford an abundance of running water the year found. Mayview is the postoffice.

are H. H. McGugin, Trustee; James W. Adams. Clerk; H. C. White. Treasurer; A. S. Clelland and J. D. Hollenbeck, Justices of the Peace, and A. G. Williams, and J. G. King, Constables.

LIMESTONE TOWNSHIP

was organized at the first meeting of the Board of County Commissioners, August 22, 1870, and was composed of Townships 3, 4 and 5, Ranges 9 and 10. It has since been reduced to one government Township (Town 3, Range 9), Athens, Erving. Ionia and Ezbon, having been formed out of its original territory.

THE FIRST ELECTION

for Township officers was held at the house of Thomas Coverdale, April 3, 1871, and resulted in the election of Adam Reimenschneider, Trustee; Seneca Sumner, Treasurer; O. S. Baxter, Clerk; John McAffee and A. D. W. Carman, Justices of the Peace, and Thomas Grimes, and C. E. Pound, Constables.

On February 12, 1874, it was organized as it now stands, with Geo. S. Vilott, Trustee; Ransom J. Harwick. Clerk, and George Snyder, Treasurer.

The Township contains six miles square of excellent rolling land, rich and productive. It is well watered by the second and third branches of Limestone creek, on which is found an abundance of good timber.

THE FIRST SETTLER

of the Township was Captain Garland, an old sea captain, who settled on the third branch of Limestone in the fall of 1870. The second batch of settlers were Robert Pattison and family, who settled on the fourth branch of Limestone, the same fall, though a little later.

The first white child born in the Township was born to Mrs. Anna Burgess, in 1871; it was also the first death, as it died a very short time after its birth, followed in a few days by its mother.

Every quarter section of land in the Township is taken, and nearly all of them contain actual settlers. The people are intelligent, moral and industrious, and the society is good. There are four school districts in the Township, in all of which regular terms of school are taught. There is only $600 bonded indebtedness in the Township. There are two church organizations in the Township—the Methodists and Presbyterians, both of which have regular preaching, and Sunday Schools. Present population—470. Ezbon is the post office.

elected November 6, 1877, are: John McCammon, Trustee; Geo. W. Congleton, Clerk; W. H. Isaacs, Treasurer; F. E. Cannon and W. P. Walker, Justices of the Peace, and A. W. Parkhurst and S. E. Maxson, Constables.

PRAIRIE TOWNSHIP

was organized April 16, 1872, being cut off from Buffalo and containing all of Township 5, Range 7, with the exception of the first tier of sections, which remained a portion of Buffalo Township until the October 1877 meeting of the Board of County Commissioners, when it was taken away from Buffalo and declared the legitimate property of Prairie. It is a beautiful, rich and fertile Township of land, and is thickly settled by an industrious, energetic and intelligent class of citizens, well and favorably known for their piety and morality. They all came here poor, but they went to work with a will and determination to make their beautiful prairie homes bloom and blossom like the rose, and we are pleased to chronicle the fact that their efforts have been crowned with entire success.

THE FIRST SETTLERS

of Prairie Township were: Wm. D. and Jonathan Street, Benjamin Lewis and J. A. Zimmerman, who came here in October 1869, and Jesse N. Carpenter and Eugene Carpenter, who came early in the spring of 1870. Wm. M. Jones, Isaac A. Sawin and Charles L. Seeley followed soon after, arriving here April 29, 1870. Wm. W. and John McCracken, the proprietors of "McCracken's Ranche," came in August 1870. A host of others came in about the same time, but our limited space forbids further particulars under this head.

SCHOOLS AND CHURCHES.

Prairie Township contains four school districts, in all of which there are good substantial school houses, in which regular terms of school are taught. The religious element is also well represented—the Methodists, Christians and Baptists, all having regular organizations and places of worship.

THE PRESENT TOWNSHIP OFFICERS, elected November 6, 1877, are: Stephen Kilgore, Trustee; J. F. Harrington, Treasurer; D. A. Salley, Clerk; E. Gard and J. B. Allen, Justices of the Peace; J. T. Whitney and J. C. Thornton, Constables.

VICKSBURG TOWNSHIP

was organized at the first meeting of the Board of County Commissioners, August 22, 1870, and was composed of Townships 3, 4 and 5, Range 6.

THE FIRST ELECTION

for Township officers took place at A. J. Davis' house, April 3, 1871, and resulted in the election of O. F. Johnson, Trustee; Thos. Dale, Treasurer; A. J. Highland, Clerk; James Fogle, Jr. and Abraham Alsdurf, Justices of the Peace; J. M. Welch and Jeremiah Burnett, Constables.

THE FIRST SETTLERS,

as the Township now stands, were: Captain O. F. Johnson, Mathias Hofweimer, Lewis Speigle, Wm. R. Friend, C. James Jones, Abraham Alsdurf, George Zimmer, James Fogle, Jr., Thomas Dale, William Taylor and Silas Mann, all of whom settled in the Township in the fall of 1870, the three first taking their claims August 11, 1870.

THE FIRST MARRIAGE

in the township took place June 17, 1871, Captain O. F. Johnson and Miss Elizabeth Zimmer being the contracting parties. This was also the first marriage in the county, standing No. 1 on the marriage record of the Probate Judge's office.

The Township is well watered by Marsh creek and its tributaries. Its present territory is township 4 south, Range 6 west, and contains six miles square of excellent table land, rich and productive. Its inhabitants are intelligent, moral and industrious. It contains four school districts, in all of which regular terms of school are taught. Every quarter section of land in the Township is taken, nearly all of which contains actual settlers. Its present population is 441.

THE PRESENT TOWNSHIP OFFICERS, elected November 6, 1877, are Edwin Wertenberger, Trustee; John Kissinger, Treasurer; J. K. Adams, Clerk; A. Alsdurf and J. K. Adams, Justices of the Peace; J. A. Bell and B. F. Hardin, Constables.

OHIO,

the only town in the Township is a thriving, enterprising little place, started in 1877. It contains a post office, two general stores, two blacksmith shops, and several handsome private residences. Johnsonville, named in honor of Captain O. F. Johnson, is a post office near the center of the Township.

BEDON TOWNSHIP

was originally a portion of Limestone Township. It was organized August 10, 1872, and at that time contained all of Township 3, south, Ranges 9 and 10, west. It now contains Township 3, south, Range 10, west.

THE FIRST SETTLERS.

of the Township, as it now stands, were Henderson Ward, John W. Ward, Levi Ward and Geo. W. Ward, who settled and took claims on the west branch of the West Branch of Limestone creek in October, 1870. Several other settlers came in that fall and the next spring, but we are unable to get the names and date of but very few. Among them were Hon. D. W. Pate, afterwards Representative; A. W. D. Carman, afterwards Justice of the Peace and S. O. Carman, afterwards Register of Deeds. The Carmans came in 1870, and Mr. Pate came in March, 1871.

THE FIRST ELECTION

held in the Township was the general election of 1872, held November 5, 1872, at which 20 votes were cast, all of them for the Republican ticket. The first Township election was held on the first day of April, 1871, at which Geo. S. Vilott was elected Trustee; C. W. Tillotson, Clerk; M. F. Rozell, Treasurer; S. C. Jackson and Gideon Brown, Justices of the Peace and Clarence E. Pound and Frank S. Griffith, Constables.

SCHOOLS AND CHURCHES.

There are four school districts in the Township, in which regular terms of school are kept. There are also four church organizations—the Catholics, Free Methodists, Dunkards and United Brethern, all of whom have Sunday Schools in connection therewith, and regular preaching. The people are intelligent, industrious, thrifty farmers, and the society is good. The Township contains six miles square of fine rolling land, rich and productive, and is well watered by Limestone and its numerous tributaries. The only

CATHOLIC CHURCH BUILDING

In the county is a neat one story stone edifice, 23x33, situated near the residence of Martin Regan, in Ezbon Township, Father Timphaus, of Beloit, Priest in charge. The building cost $600, is nicely finished, and is a credit to the county.

THE PRESENT TOWNSHIP OFFICERS, elected November 6, 1877, are: Martin Regan, Trustee; N. Z. Lewis, Clerk; Henry Hershner, Treasurer; J. C. Hubbard and Percival Sheard, Justices of the Peace; P. G. Regan and S. C. Jackson, Constables.

ATHENS TOWNSHIP

was originally a portion of Limestone Township. It was organized August 19, 1872, and the first election was held at the house of T. B. Johns, August 28, 1872, which resulted in the election of E. D. Plumb, Justice of the Peace; Thomas B. Johns, Township Treasurer, and Robert Day and Jacob Gilmore, Constables. No other Township officers were elected at this time. John McAffee, Justice of the Peace, and A. S. Hoag, Township Clerk, who had been appointed, held over until the next regular election.

THE FIRST SETTLERS

of Athens Township were Fred Beeler, E. D. Plumb, Richard Albertson, Robert White, John McAffee, all of whom came onto Limestone creek in April 1870.

SCHOOLS AND CHURCHES.

There are four School Districts in the Township, all of which have school houses, and regular terms of school. The religious denominations are Methodists, Presbyterians and Dunkards, all of whom have regular preaching.

The people are moral, intellegent, industrious and prosperous, and the society is unsurpassed.

Athens Township is one of the finest Townships of land in the county and is well watered by Limestone creek and its tributaries, which afford an abundance of running water the year round, and is bordered by a wide belt of excellent timber.

THE PRESENT TOWNSHIP OFFICERS, elected November 6, 1877, are Morris Gray, Trustee; J. C. Slagle, Clerk; Geo. B. Steen, Treasurer; M. B. Barton and Charles Stoner, Justices of the Peace, and John Yantis and D. C. Slagle, Constables.

ERVING TOWNSHIP

was originally a portion of Limestone. It is situated in the southwest corner of Jewell county, and comprises Township 5 south, Range 10 west. It was organized November 10, 1872, and named in honor of Dr. Erving, of Hiawatha, Kansas, from which place quite a number of the first settlers emigrated.

THE FIRST ELECTION

took place April 3, 1873, at which Fred J. Vosburg was elected Trustee. The records fail to show the election of any other officers. Perhaps the people were just as well off without them.

THE FIRST SETTLERS.

Fred J. Vosburg took the first claim in the township in June 1870. He was followed in the spring of 1871 by Wm. Babcock, Frank Clark, R. Snider, Al. Chandler, George Engleheart, F. J. Heller, Peter De Young, George Schoonmaker, Henry Van Tilborg and a great many others. In fact so great was the rush of emigration that spring that before the close of 1871, all the land in the Township was taken up. The Township is well watered by Oak creek and its tributaries along the banks of which an abundance of excellent timber is found. The soil is rich and productive.

SCHOOLS AND CHURCHES.

There are three School Districts, in two of which are good substantial school houses, in which regular terms of school are taught. The other district contemplates building this fall. The church organizations are—the Dutch Reformed Church, who have a commodious church building and parsonage; the Advents and the Congregationalists. The two latter have no church buildings, but all have regular preaching. The majority of the inhabitants are Hollanders. They are honest, industrious, hardworking people, and make good citizens.

THE PRESENT TOWNSHIP OFFICERS, elected November 6, 1877, are: Henry Van Tilborg, Trustee; R. W. Mayrihugh, Clerk; George Schoonmaker, Treasurer; Fred J. Vosburg and F. J. Heller, Justices of the Peace, and William Orchard and Geo. M. Stanton, Constables.

WHITE MOUND TOWNSHIP

was originally a portion of White Rock Township, which was organized August 22, 1870, the date of the county's organization. It now comprises Township 2 south, Range 10 west. Organized January 7, 1873

THE FIRST SETTLERS were Nelson Frost, John Brittan, H. C. Bachelder, and Wesley Clemens, who took claims on White Rock in June 1870. The next settler was Menzo W. Smith, who came in July 1870. The next settlers were W. H. McKimmey, the first and present township trustee, J. B. Aringdale and A. J. Dodd, who took their claims on the 7th day of October, 1870.

THE FIRST ELECTION held in the township was at Salem, November 5th, 1872. The result of the election was very satisfactory to the Republican party, every vote cast being for the Republican ticket.

THE FIRST TOWNSHIP OFFICERS, appointed by the county commissioners were: W. H. McKimmey, trustee; Geo. W. C. Smith, clerk; James Cline, treasurer, and Menzo W. Smith, justice of the peace. No constables

were appointed. Mr. Smith did not find out that he was not a legally constituted justice of the peace until after he had performed his first marriage ceremony. He was afterwards legally appointed justice of the peace by Gov. Osborn.

THE FIRST ELECTION held in the township for township officers, was held at Salem, April 1, 1873, at which 41 votes were cast, resulting in the election of W. H. McKimmey, trustee; Thos. L. Guthrie, Clerk; James Mounce, treasurer; Menzo W. Smith and James Campbell, justices of the peace, and Isaac Conger and Samuel Frazier, constables.

The first white child born in White Mound Township was a girl born to Mr. and Mrs. A. J. Dodd, August 24, 1871. Her name is Mattie; she is a bright little girl, and is still living with her parents on the old original homestead.

The first and only steam mill in the township was started by H. L. Browning, February 1, 1872. It is still running at Salem, and has done an immense amount of good in the improvement of the township. H. L. Browning located the claim on which he is now living, August 5, 1871. On December 12, 1871, he returned and settled permanently, bringing his steam saw mill with him.

Menzo W. Smith was the first settler in the immediate neighborhood of the present town of Salem, being for some time the farthest settler west in Jewell county, or Northwestern Kansas. Mr. Smith still remains an honored resident of the township, and is justice of the peace and Postmaster at Salem.

SCHOOLS AND CHURCHES.

There are seven school districts, three of them, however, lapping over into other townships. There are school houses in all the districts but two, and regular terms of school are taught in all. There is no bonded indebtedness in any of them. There are six church organizations—Free Will Methodists, United Brethren, Christians, Dunkards, Quakers and Spiritualists. A union meeting house is in course of construction on the northwest corner of W. H. McKinmey's claim, which is to be used by all denominations for preaching and Sunday Schools.

White Mound Township contains six miles square of as fine land as there is in the county, all of which is well watered by White Rock and its numerous tributaries, on all of which an abundance of excellent native timber is found. It is thickly settled by an industrious, intelligent and active class of citizens, and the society is good.

THE PRESENT TOWNSHIP OFFICERS, elected November 6, 1877, are: W. H. McKinmey, trustee; James Brown, clerk; H. L. Browning, treasurer; Menzo W. Smith and John Hill, justices of the peace, and F. D. Joy and Thomas Sheard, constables.

SALEM,

the only town in the township, is a busy, bustling and enterprising little town full of business and in the enjoyment of an excellent trade. It was laid out January 25, 1872, by H. L. Browning, C. P. Miller and Geo. W. Smith, the town site being a strip of ground taken from each one of their claims. The first store house was built by Browning and Smith in March 1872, which was occupied for a short time by Wilson Brothers, of Scandia, with a small stock of goods. The first permanent store was opened here by J. M. Parker, June 1, 1872, who done a big mercantile business for a long time, and is now engaged in the stock business. Miller and Smith have both left the county. Miller is preaching for the Free Methodists near Galesburg, Illinois, and Smith is engaged in the same laudable calling for the same denomination at Council Grove, Kansas. Browning has not yet commenced preaching. All branches of business are well represented in Salem, as evidence of which we refer with pleasure to the numerous "cards" of that town to be found in our advertising pages.

RICHLAND TOWNSHIP

was originally a portion of Big Timber. Was organized as Richland Township, February 12, 1874.

ITS FIRST OFFICERS

were: Andrew Green, Trustee; C. P.

B. Dazy, Treasurer; John W. McRoberts, Jr. and T. McBride, Justices of the Peace, and John Wyatt, Constable.

THE FIRST SETTLERS

were Sam. C. Bowles, T. Bowles, G. I. Nelson, Peter Kearns, Peter Tanner, Nels Cederburg, John O'Roak, Chris. Ahrens, John W. McRoberts, Sr., John W. McRoberts, Jr. W. R. Scott, Sam. J. Sweet, Alfred Wilde and Urban Wilde, all of whom settled here early in the spring of 1870, some of them coming in February and the remainder in April.

The Township is a little inclined to be rolling, but as its name indicates, the land is rich and productive. It is well watered by John's and White Rock creeks, and good timber is abundant. It is thickly settled by an industrious and thrifty class of farmers, and the society is good.

SCHOOLS AND CHURCHES.

There are four school districts in the township, all of which have good school houses, in which regular terms of school are taught. We have no report of churches.

RUBENS

is a thriving little town, containing one general store, a card of which will be found in our advertising pages, a post office, in which confectioneries and notions are kept, and a blacksmith and wagon-maker's shop.

THE PRESENT TOWNSHIP OFFICERS, elected November 6, 1877, are Thomas E. West, trustee; Samuel J. Sweet, clerk; S. M. Wright, treasurer; W. G. King and W. Wilde, justices of the peace, and W. S. Wright and W. J. Bowles, Constables.

CALVIN TOWNSHIP

was the last township organized in the county—December 7, 1875. It was originally a portion of Buffalo. It is well watered by Middle and West Buffalo, and is a splendid township of land. It was named in honor of J. Calvin Postlethwaite, who was mainly instrumental in its organization. Thickly settled; society good.

THE FIRST SETTLERS

were Henry Sorick, Geo. A. Sorick, James A. Scarbrough and William Queen, all of whom settled here in

April 1870. The next settlers were Col. E. Barker, F. T. Gandy, Lewis Gandy, Orville L. McClung, and W. C. McClung, who settled in May and June 1870. William M. Runyan was the *first settler* of West Prairie in this township, settling here in August 1870.

THE FIRST TOWNSHIP OFFICERS

were: F. T. Gandy, trustee; John Delong, clerk; A. Wyland, treasurer; A. Jackson and T. J. Casson, justices of the peace, and Oliver Majers and J. F. Schoonover, constables.

SCHOOLS AND CHURCHES.

There are two school districts in the township, both of which have good school houses and regular terms of school. Having for a long time been attached to Buffa' nd Centre townships, nearly all the School Districts had been formed before it was organized as an independent township. Hence the best portion of its territory is thrown into these townships for school purposes. There are two church organizations—the Methodists and Evangelicals, both of which have regular preaching and Sunday Schools.

THE PRESENT TOWNSHIP OFFICERS,

elected November 6, 1877, are: A. Harbour, trustee; H. S. Cox, clerk; R. R. McClung, treasurer; A. Jackson and G. W. McGehee, justices of the peace, and H. Pitkin and James Barton, constables. Judge Jackson has since removed to Missouri Valley, Iowa.

JACKSON TOWNSHIP

was originally a portion of Big Timber township, and was organized April 16, 1872.

THE FIRST ELECTION

took place May 14, 1872, at which A. W. Vale was elected trustee; Milton Ringland, clerk; M. Jennings, treasurer; G. W. Byers and A. B. Marsh, justices of the peace, and R. A. Badley and John Maudlin, constables.

THE FIRST SETTLERS

were Frank Bregren, S. E. Wilson and Walker Vale, who came in 1870, and G. W. Byers, M. Jennings, A. B. French, H. A. French and Andrew

Eisenmann, who settled in the spring of 1871.

Jackson township is situated in the extreme northeast corner of the county, and consists of Township 1, south, Range 6, west. It contains six miles square of fine rolling land, the north half sloping towards the Republican river, and the south half towards White Rock creek. That portion lying immediately along the Republican embraces a beautiful tract of rich bottom land. The people as a class will compare favorable with any other community in the county, in point of intelligence, industry, sociability and morals.

SCHOOLS AND CHURCHES.

There are four school districts in the township, all of which have comfortable school houses, in which regular terms of school are taught. There are two church organizations— the Baptists and United Brethren— each of which have regular preaching and Sabbath Schools.

THE PRESENT TOWNSHIP OFFICERS,

elected November 6, 1877, are M. Jennings, trustee; W. G. Whiting, clerk; John Hobson, treasurer; R. M. Clark and G. W. Higgins, justices of the peace, and A. L. Skeels and H. A. French, constables.

IONIA TOWNSHIP

was originally a portion of Limestone township, and nearly all the "first township officers" mentioned in Limestone township are now residents of Ionia. As it now stands it consists of Township 4, south, Ranges 9 and 10, west, and was organized August 10, 1872, and is the largest township in the county.

THE FIRST TOWNSHIP OFFICERS,

elected August 28, 1872, were William Roney, trustee; S. O. Carman, clerk, and J. Webster, justice of the peace, each of whom received 6 votes. As they were loyal, law-abiding people they elected no treasurer or constable.

THE FIRST SETTLERS

were O. S. Baxter, Thomas Grimes, Erving Wooster, O. H. P. Cook, M. V. Smith, E. S. Wright, B. M. Curtis, L. E. Ransom and James W.

Moses, all of whom took claims in the months of August and September 1870, the first six in August and the others in September. Frank L. Pound came in in November, 1870.

A. N. Cole homesteaded the first claim in the township, September, 29, 1869, but left it and never returned for nearly a year afterwards—September 20, 1870. Adam Riemenschnider and wife came in with Cole and settled near where they now live. Mr. R., had been out the previous spring and homesteaded his claim March 1, 1870.

The east half of Ionia township is thickly settled and one of the best sections of land in the west. The land is rich and productive, and is well watered and timbered—Ash creek and the four main branches of Limestone creek traversing it from north to south. The west half is rather hilly and thinly settled. However there is some good land on the east branch of Oak creek, and the thick settlement of the entire township is only a question of time. The people are intelligent, industrious and sociable, and the society is good.

SCHOOLS AND CHURCHES.

There are four school districts in the township, all of which have good substantial school houses, in which regular terms of school are taught. There are three church organizations —the Methodists, Presbyterians and Dunkards—all of which have regular preaching and Sunday Schools.

IONIA

is a flourishing little town, located in the southern part of the township, containing two general stores, one boot and shoe shop and one blacksmith shop. It is beautifully located near the middle forks of Limestone creek, and is a place of considerable trade. Being surrounded by a rich and fertile country its future is bright and promising.

THE PRESENT TOWNSHIP OFFICERS, elected November 6, 1877, are James V. Davis, trustee; E. H. Colson, clerk; Geo. Barnett, treasurer; H. C. Davis and Stephen Hoffhines, justices of the peace, and F. F. Finch and C. Rindom, constables.

BURR OAK TOWNSHIP

is the legitimate successor of White Rock township, all the first officers of the latter being now residents of the former. As before mentioned in this work White Rock township was organized August 22, 1870.

ITS FIRST OFFICERS,

elected April, 3, 1871, were Jabe Winslow, Trustee; Frank Gilbert, treasurer; James McCormick, clerk; Thomas Moor and A. W. Mann, justices of the peace, and J. K. Moor and Zack Mormon, constables.

THE FIRST SETTLERS

were A. W. Mann, A. J. Godfrey, D. H. Godfrey, Frank Gilbert, James Gilbert, George Beanblossom, Sr., Mike Hackenberg, John St. John, and Thomas Francis, who settled near the present town site of Burr Oak, August 28, 1870. A. W. Mann had been out in June previous and had taken his claim. Of the nine persons above named all remain, with the exception of Thomas Francis and John St. John, who have moved away, and Mike Hackenberg who was killed on his claim by the falling of a tree in the fall of 1874. Zack Mormon and Thomas R. Comstock came in September, 1870.

Thomas Moor and J. K. Moor, and Henry Sprague came in about the 1st of October, 1870, and took claims on Burr Oak creek, about five miles northwest of Burr Oak, where they still reside.

John E. Faidley and Allen Ives came out and took a look at the country in October, 1870, but did not take claims. They came back in January, 1871, to find the nice claims they had selected on their first visit taken by other parties.

BURR OAK.

The beautiful town site of Burr Oak was located and laid out by A. J. Godfrey, on the NW ¼ of the NW ¼ of Section 23, Township 2, south, Range 9, west, in May 1872. John E. Faidley built the first house and opened the first store in this place, in the same month, which was the beginning of the present town of Burr Oak, which now contains two good general stores, one drug store, one harness shop, one water saw and grist mill, one sewing and reaping machine establishment and two good hotels.

On the 23rd day of May, 1873, Mr. Faidley took Francis Gilbert into partnership with him and the firm was known as Faidley & Gilbert until March 18th, 1878, when they went into partnership with A. W. Mann, and the firm is now known as Mann, Faidley & Co.

Barr Oak township is one of the best in the county, and is thickly settled by as good a class of citizens as ever came west. Population 639.

SCHOOLS AND CHURCHES.

There are six school districts in the township, all of which have good school houses and regular terms of school. There are three Sunday Schools. The religic denominations are quite numerous, and are represented as follows: Methodists, Friends, United Brethren, Dunkards, Saturday and Sunday Advents, Christians, Presbyterians and Spiritualists, all of whom have regular preaching.

THE PRESENT TOWNSHIP OFFICERS,

elected November 6, 1877, are J. W. Green, trustee; A. J. Godfrey, clerk; B. F. Royer, Treasurer; James McCormick and J. M. Quigley, justices of the peace, and David H. Godfrey, and A. Morris, constables.

WASHINGTON TOWNSHIP

was originally a portion of Buffalo Township. It was organized August 10, 1872, and

THE FIRST ELECTION

took place at the house of Captain Pierce, August 28, 1872, at which C. Stinson was elected Trustee; W. G. Slaughter, Treasurer; A. P. Huling, Clerk; S. Briggs, Justice of the Peace, and A. Walker and J. L. Allen, Constables.

THE FIRST SETTLERS

were J. M. Pantier, B. M. Gould, J. L. Allen, Seth Rogers and W. G Slaughter, who settled on West Marsh creek the first of May, 1871. The first child born was to Mr. and Mrs. J. L. Allen, November 10, 1871.

The eastern portion of the Township contains some beautiful country,

as fine as any in the county, but the western port: n is rather broken and hilly, but all susceptable of successful cultivation. The Township is thickly settled by industrious, intelligent and successful farmers, and the society is excellent.

SCHOOLS AND CHURCHES.

There are four school districts, in all of which there are regular terms of school. There are five church organizations—Presbyterians, Methodists, Christians, United Brethren and Free Will Baptists, all of whom have regular preaching. J. M. Pantier is Pastor of the Presbyterian church, and J. L. Allen, class leader of the Methodists.

THE PRESENT TOWNSHIP OFFICERS,

elected November 6, 1877, are W. G. Slaughter, Trustee; Jacob Jacobs, Clerk; J. L. Allen, Treasurer; J. M Adams and Geo. Keyes, Justices of the Peace, and L. B. Jordan and J. Jacobs, Constables.

GRANT TOWNSHIP

was originally a portion of Vicksburg Township. It is a splendid Township of land and is well watered by East and Middle Marsh creeks, on whose banks is found an abundance of excellent timber. The land is all taken up, and is settled by a moral, industrious and intelligent class of citizens.

THE FIRST SETTLERS

were James Fogle, Jr., J. Sturdevant, D. Nickerson, Mr. Brassfield and James Fogle, Sr., all of whom came in in April, 1871, with the exception of James Fogle, Jr., who arrived in March, 1871, and who may be justly regarded as the *first settler*. The Township was organized April 8, 1873.

THE FIRST ELECTION

took place April 22, 1873, at the house of E. Bullock, at which C. Stinson was elected Trustee; B. Hobson, Clerk; W. Orton, Treasurer, and S. McCay, Justice of the Peace.

SCHOOLS AND CHURCHES.

There are six school districts in the Township, in all of which there are good substantial school houses, in which regular terms of school are taught. The church organizations number six, as follows: Methodists,

Advents, Christians, Presbyterians, Baptists and United Brethren, all of whom have regular preaching.

THE PRESENT TOWNSHIP OFFICERS held over from last year, there being no election in the township last fall. Captain A. B. Balch is Trustee and Justice of the Peace. The names of the other officers we were unable to obtain.

SINCLAIR TOWNSHIP

was originally a portion of Big Timber Township. It is situated on White Rock creek, on the eastern line of the county, immediately west of White Rock City. Much of its early history will be found in the opening chapters of this work. It is a splendid Township of land and is thickly settled by a good class of citizens. It was organized February 12, 1874, and its

FIRST TOWNSHIP OFFICERS

were John Dixon, Trustee; R. A. Badley, Clerk; H. C. Vestal, Treasurer; John Renshaw, Justice of the Peace, and R. A. Badley and T. Hunter, Constables.

THE FIRST SETTLERS

were C. G. Smith, Allen D. Woodruff and Mrs. Mary Frazier and her two sons Frank and William—who settled here in 1866; Thomas Shuler, Willard Woodruff, William Nixon, James Clelland, Hugh Clelland, Ed. Hanner, Joel Friend, H. Lapier, James McCraith, Eli Thomas and E. Mauldin, who settled in 1870.

SCHOOLS AND CHURCHES.

There are four school districts in the township, in all of which there are good substantial school houses, in which regular terms of school are taught. There are three church organizations—the United Brethren, Presbyterians and Methodists, all of whom have regular preaching and Sunday Schools.

THE PRESENT TOWNSHIP OFFICERS, elected November 6, 1877, are A. H. Poole, Trustee; A. L. Milligan, Clerk; H. C. Vestal, treasurer; Ed. Hanner and F. M. Poole, justices of the peace, and R. A. Clelland and T. J. Hutchison, constables.

MONTANA TOWNSHIP

was originally a portion of Big Timber. It is rather high and rolling, but the north half, sloping gracefully towards the Republican river, contains some beautiful bottom land. A tributary of White Rock creek drains the south half of the township, on which there is also some splendid land. It is all rich and productive, even the upland being very desirable. It is thickly settled by an industrious and intelligent class of citizens, and the society is good.

THE FIRST SETTLERS.

Adam Rosenberg, the Indian fighter of former chapters of this little book, was *the first settler* of Montana. Ed. Davis, Frank Wilson and McCracken are 1870 settlers, but the great rush of immigration to this township was in 1871. Wm. O. Ebersole, Geo. Lowe, Taylor Davis and Joseph Blair were among the early settlers of this township. February 12, 1874, the township was organized, and

THE FIRST TOWNSHIP OFFICERS

were M. D. Ross, trustee; A. G. Nunnally, clerk; John Lane, treasurer; S. M. Wright, justice of the peace, and John Gatewood and John Blair, constables.

SCHOOLS AND CHURCHES.

Montana township contains three school districts, all of which have good comfortable school houses, in which regular terms of school are taught. We have no report of churches.

THE PRESENT TOWNSHIP OFFICERS, elected November 6, 1877, are D. C. Wilson, trustee; W. L. Ross, treasurer; J. K. Pratt, clerk; H. C. Boder and W. H. Haskinson, justices of the peace, and F. W. Broeaw and S. T. McBride, constables.

HARRISON TOWNSHIP

lays on the divide between the Republican river and White Rock creek. The surface of the country is rolling, sloping to the north and south. It is well watered by Ash, Oak, Augur and Crooked creeks, running north, and Hoag, Knob, Norway and Taylor creeks, running south, on nearly all of which there is considerable timber. The township is thickly settled by a

good class of citizens and the society
is excellent.

THE FIRST SETTLERS

were George Harrison, James Marion,
Isaac Donahoe, John McClure, Geo.
S. Hill, Morris Morrison and Martin
Morrison, the first two coming in
February and the remainder in April,
1871. The township was originally
one-half in White Rock and the oth-
er half in Big Timber. It was organ-
ized as an independent township
April 13, 1874.

THE FIRST TOWNSHIP OFFICERS

were Peter Van Orman, trustee; G.
M. Jacobs, treasurer and A. O. Bacon,
clerk.

SCHOOLS AND CHURCHES.

There are six school districts, in
five of which there are school houses,
in which regular terms of school are
taught. There are three church organizations—the Bible Christians,
Methodists and German Methodists,
all of whom have regular preaching.
There are three Union Sunday
Schools, all in a flourishing condition.

THE PRESENT TOWNSHIP OFFICERS

elected November 6, 1877, are J. M.
Armagost, trustee; James Essex,
clerk, H. B. Forrey, treasurer; J. C.
Armagost and D. S. Kenney, justices
of the peace, and D. A. Rogers and A.
Buttler, constables.

WALNUT TOWNSHIP

lays on the divide between the Republican river and White Rock
creek; it is principally upland and
considerably broken, but is neverthe-
less, rich and productive. There is
considerable timber on the different
streams, the principal of which is
Walnut, from which the township
takes its name. It is thickly settled
by intelligent, industrious farmers,
and the society is good.

THE FIRST SETTLERS

were J. G. Moon and A. J. Sprague,
who settled here in the spring of 1870.
The next were J. T. Hollenbeck, John
Green, A. B. George, Abel Carter,
Enoch Scott and Job Williams,
who settled in 1871.

Walnut was originally a portion of
White Rock township. It was organized as an independent township February 12, 1874.

THE FIRST ELECTION

was held April 7, 1874, at which H. C.
Huntington was elected trustee; O.
F. Roberts, (now County Commissioner) clerk; J. T. Hollenbeck, treasurer; D. Richmond and J. P. Cole,
justices of the peace, and A. C. Cox
and O. B. Ford, constables.

SCHOOLS AND CHURCHES.

There are five school districts in the
township, three of which have good
school houses. The other two hold
school in houses erected for meeting
houses. Regular terms of school are
taught in all the districts. There are
two church organizations—the United
Brethren, and Quakers or Friends,
both of which have regular preaching.
There are three Union Sunday
Schools, all in a flourishing condition.

THE PRESENT TOWNSHIP OFFICERS

elected November 6, 1877, are A. A.
Davis, trustee; E. Gardner, clerk; D.
R. Dillon, treasurer; E. B. Ensign
and J. T. Hollenbeck, justices of the
peace, and G. Flynn and O. P. Ma-
honey, constables.

HIGHLAND TOWNSHIP

is situated in the extreme northwest
corner of the county. It was originally a portion of White Mound, but
was erected into an independent
township February 12, 1874. The
most of the township is high rolling
upland, but is rich and productive.
It is well watered by Ash and Amity
creeks, along whose banks considerable timber is found. Every quarter-
section of land in the township is
taken and nearly all contain actual
settlers. The people are highly intelligent, and the society good.

THE FIRST SETTLERS

were William Gettys, J. R. Lyman,
James Mitchell, R. W. Bullock and
Harrison Davis, all of whom settled
here in 1871. William Gettys was
the *first* settler, coming in April 1871,
the others during the summer and
fall of that year.

THE FIRST ELECTION

was held April 7, 1874, at which W.
M. Wright was elected trustee; J. F.
Webb, clerk; G. W. S. Micheals, treas-

urer; Joseph Blair and Elbridge Hill, justices of the peace, and P. N. Hogue and A. D. Brown, constables.

There are six school districts in the township, all of which have good school houses and regular terms of school. There are three church organizations—the United Presbyterians, United Brethren, and Methodists, all of which have regular preaching and Sunday schools. The United Presbyterians have a nice stone church building 24x36.

THE PRESENT TOWNSHIP OFFICERS, elected November 6, 1877, are Elbridge Hill, trustee; E. E. Shute, clerk; E. C. Smith, treasurer; Sylvester Hill and Joseph Blair, justices of the peace, and A. N. Patmore and G. H. Simpson, constables.

HOLMWOOD TOWNSHIP

lays immediately on White Rock creek, and is one of the best Townships in the county. There is plenty of good timber and good water. It is thickly settled by a good class of citizens, and the society is unsurpassed. It was organized January 7, 1873.

THE FIRST TOWNSHIP OFFICERS

were: John A. Robertson, Trustee; M. Farnham, Clerk; J. B. Scripture, Treasurer; John A. Gates and Wm. Ireland, Justices of the Peace, and William Hess and David Korb, Constables.

SCHOOLS AND CHURCHES.

There are four school districts in the Township, in all of which there are good substantial school houses, in which regular terms of school are taught. We have no report of churches, or first settlers.

HOLMWOOD

is a thriving little town on White Rock creek, and is a place of considerable trade.

THE PRESENT TOWNSHIP OFFICERS,

elected November 6, 1877, are: D. M. Callender, Trustee; John A. Robertson, Clerk; Geo. W. Sterling, Treasurer; John A. Gates and W. B. Williams, Justices of the Peace, and W. G. Hunter and William Robertson, Constables.

CENTRE TOWNSHIP

is located in the geographical centre of Jewell county, and is composed of Township 3 south, Range 8 west. Although rather rough and broken, the soil is excellent, and the land is all taken up. The Township is drained by the Middle Branch of Buffalo creek, on which there is an abundance of good timber and fine building stone. It is thickly settled by a good class of citizens, and the society is equal to any in the west.

THE FIRST SETTLERS.

H. C. Ussher, now of Grand Round Valley, Oregon, was *the first settler* of Center Township, taking his claim on Middle Buffalo in July, 1870. The next settler was Jack Vingo, who took the claim now owned by David S. Blank, in August, 1870. S. R. Worick took the claim which he now owns, in May 1870, but made no permanent settlement until 1871. January 19, 1871, Ruben Worick came out and took the claim on which he now lives. He came back with his family in June, 1871, and has remained here ever since. David S. Blank came out in June, 1872, and bought out Jack Vingo. About this time the

JEWELL CENTRE TOWN COMPANY

was organized, and the present town site of Jewell Centre was filed on and the town laid out. The officers of the company were: N. W. Whitney, President; P. S. McCutchen, Secretary, and Geo. S. Bishop, Treasurer.

THE FIRST BUILDING

erected on the town site was a blacksmith shop, put up by David S. Blank. The next was the present court house, erected by the Town Company and afterwards presented to the county for a court house.

THE FIRST STORE

was opened in Jewell Centre by Chas. W. Pettigrew, November 20, 1872. Other buildings followed in rapid succession, and immigration was unprecedented. By April 1, 1873, the town had grown to such dimensions that the residents concluded they would give Jewell City a tussle for

THE COUNTY SEAT.

Consequently a petition to that effect was presented to the County Commissioners, April 7, 1873, and an election was ordered to come off May 13, 1873. The result of that election was that the county seat was moved to Jewell Centre by a vote of 861 to 626 for Jewell City, being a majority of 235 in favor of Jewell Centre. After this county seat matters remained quiet until June 28, 1875, when another election took place for the re-location of the county seat. The result was 971 for Jewell Centre; 756 for Jewell City, and 9 for Midway, another "imaginary town," on Middle Buffalo. The majority this time in favor of Jewell Centre was 206. Since the last county seat election the town has improved wonderfully, and is now second to none in the county. Our space forbids a more lengthy notice in this place. The long list of cards in our advertising columns will give our readers a very fair idea of the population and business.

Centre Township was organized August 10, 1872, and

THE FIRST ELECTION

took place August 28, 1872, at which S. F. Scripture was elected Clerk; A. M. Brinkerhoff, Treasurer; D. J. Vance and Geo. A. Sorick, Justices of the Peace, and R. F. Hudsonpeller and Richard Chilcott, Constables.

SCHOOLS AND CHURCHES.

There are four school districts in the Township, all of which have good comfortable school houses and regular terms of school. There are three church organizations—Methodists, Baptists and Presbyterians, all of whom have regular preaching and Sunday Schools. The Presbyterian church was organized February 16, 1877, and now numbers 22 members. They also have a church building in Jewell Centre nearly completed, 20x40. Rev. A. R. Naylor, Pastor in charge.

THE PRESENT TOWNSHIP OFFICERS,

elected November 6, 1877, are: S. A. Metz, Trustee; H. E. White, Clerk; L. J. Gould, Treasurer; William Doty and John Fulton, Justices of the Peace and James John and W. A. Helman, Constables.

FIRST THINGS.

A. J. Davis was the first settler on Buffalo creek, having settled on the claim where he now resides in May 1869.

The first white child born in Jewell county was born to Mr. and Mrs. Eli Thomas, of Sinclair Township, August 6, 1870.

Henry Sorick was the first County Treasurer of Jewell county. Elected September 27, 1870. Served until October 1, 1871.

The first official bond approved in Jewell county, was that of James A. Scarorough, County Clerk, approved January 2, 1871.

The first sale of school land in the county was the sale of Section 36, Township 4 south, Range 8 west, granted January 2, 1871.

The first Sunday School in Jewell county was organized and carried on in Hoffer's Grove and at Wm. H. Cameron's house in the summer of 1871.

The first school taught in Jewell county was by Wm. H. Cameron, in his own house one fourth of a mile east of Jewell City, during the summer of 1871.

The first county order allowed and issued in the county was in favor of Joseph W. Fogel, Deputy Sheriff, for $12.50, for posting election notices, allowed January 2, 1871.

The first post-office in Jewell county was called Garley, now Jewell. John Hoffer was the first postmaster, and the first mail received was from Lake Sibley, Cloud county, Kansas, July 1, 1870.

The first public prayer ever made in Jewell county was by J. C. Postlethwaite, at Fort Jewell, July 4th, 1870, on the occasion of the first celebration of our Nation's birth day in this county.

James McCormick, of White Rock, now Burr Oak Township, was the first Township Clerk in Jewell county whose bond was approved. Elected November 8, 1870. Bond approved February 20, 1871.

The old Pioneer Drug Store was occupied by Street & Scarbrough for three years, when they closed out, and the house has since been occupied by Townsdin & Gastineau, Hutchison & Co., B. E. Gastineau, and Angel & Fay, respectively, for groceries, drugs, stoves and tinware.

Maj. John M. Crowell, Special Agent of the Postoffice Department, made his first visit to Jewell City and Jewell county in September 1870.

The first article of Merchandise ever sold in Jewell county, was 20 cents worth of plug tobacco, sold by James A. Scarbrough to Wm. K. Van Horn, in Jewell City, June 30th, 1870.

The first two crops of wheat raised in Jewell county, and threshed with a threshing machine, were raised by Fred Beeler, on Limestone, and James A. Scarbrough, on Buffalo creek, in 1871. Beeler had 19 acres and Scarbrough 10 acres. Jointly they chartered a threshing machine from Delphos, Ottawa county, 60 miles away, Beeler paying a bonus of $30 and 10 cents per bushel, and Scarbrough paying a bonus of $20 and 10 cents per bushel for threshing.

JEWELL CITY.

In our history of the organization of the county, we left Jewell City on the 22nd day of August, 1870, with only three houses on the town site. Several other buildings were erected that fall, and the succeeding spring, when building became general, and business of all kinds was lively. John D. Robertson opened his general store, June 4, 1871, which was the first general store in the county. James Kelsey settled here in September, 1871, and commenced the erection of the Jewell House, which was the first hotel in the county. Judge J. W. George bought out Mrs. Dodge in October 1871, enlarged the house by building a two story addition, and erecting a large livery barn.

Geo. W. Angel came to Jewell City in March 1871, and contracted for the erection of the large hardware store afterwards occupied by him and Pat Fay; now by John D. Robertson. Mr. Angel returned in September and opened his store. Pat Fay came out in June 1872, and from that time until the present, the firm has been known as Angel & Fay.

A. L. Marks came out in June 1872, and in August of the same year opened a small jewelry and notion store. Little by little he added to his stock, until in July 1875, he opened out with a full stock of general merchandise in partnership with his brother-in-law, Adolph Hirsch, under the firm name of Marks & Hirsch. Mr. Marks is one of Jewell City's most public spirited citizens, and has done more for the permanent improvement of the town than any other man of his means within its limits.

R. W. Hill came out in February 1876, and has been very successful in trade. March 26, 1878, he occupied his present elegant and commodious quarters. He carries an immense stock of goods, and is one of our most careful and experienced business men; is clever, accommodating and liberal, and is meeting with deserved success. See full page "ad."

J. D. Robertson has no superior, and we speak of him with pride as a business man. Besides handling an immense stock of general merchandise, he deals in cattle, hogs and grain. See "ad."

Geo. B. Crandall came to Jewell City in August 1872, and opened a small drug store. He now occupies a new and elegant store on the west side of the public square, and is a worthy and influential citizen.

The Stone Drug Store on the east side of the public square, is one of the oldest establishments of the kind in the county. It is presided over by that prince of good fellows—John M. Hutchison.

All other branches of business are well represented. J. C. Osborn and A. W. Berry, each carry on the saddle and harness business.—H. F. Stone carries on the furniture business.—When you want to get your old gun repaired or a new one made, call on John S. Henninger. He is a gunsmith of forty years' experience, and thoroughly understands his business.—S. R. Worick is Postmaster and Notary Public, and deals in notions, pocket cutlery and confectionary.—Jewell City contains two good hotels

—the Jewell House, P. Meadows, proprietor, and the Kelsey House, James Kelsey, proprietor. Their "ads" will be found in our advertising pages.

Joseph W. Fogel, one of the old "Buffalo Pioneers," is one of the best stone masons in the county.—The medical profession is well represented by Drs. Geo. S. Christ and O. W. Hughes. They are both gentlemen of ability and experience.—The last firm on the list is ourselves. We carry on a general real estate agency; see our card on cover.

There are other well conducted business firms not mentioned. We owe it to those who have helped us in this work to mention their names, and in order to do so, have added several pages.

On the 24th day of March 1872, W. P. Day, assisted by W. D. Jenkins, now of the Smith county *Pioneer*, and a stirring young man, commenced the publication of a four column paper called the Jewell City CLARION. In February 1873, he sold to M. Winsor, one of the authors of this book, who continued the publication of the CLARION until May 1, 1873, when he enlarged it to a seven column paper and changed the name to the Jewell County DIAMOND.

Jewell City may now be justly regarded as one of the rising young towns of the west. It contains two completed church buildings, and tw more are in course of construction. It has one lodge of Free Masons and one of Odd Fellows; both flourishing. Its society is equal to any in the west.

WHITE ROCK CITY.

This town is located in the beautiful valley of the stream from which it takes its name, in Republic county, though adjoining Jewell. It derives a large share of its trade from Jewell, and several of its business men reside in Jewell. It is the largest town on White Rock creek, containing 250 inhabitants. It has four stores, two hotels, two blacksmith shops, one harness shop, one boot and shoe shop. The business men are S. E. & S. R.

Morlan, general merchandise, also hardware and tin shop, in a separate building, under the management of J. S. Tippery. Charles Parian, general merchandise, is an "old reliable." Crouch & Bros., have just started in general merchandise. H. K. Peckham, druggest, Geo. Caswell, boots & shoes, Geo. B. Smith, harness and saddles, Jonathan Tippery and D. C. Badley, each have a blacksmith shop. Wm. Carman, wagon maker, J. Z. Scott M. D., physician and surgeon. Mrs. Geo. Caswell and Mrs. Chester Babcock, each supply millinery. Shuler & Leigh are Attorneys-at-Law, Real Estate and Collection Agents. Mr. Shuler is one of the Commissioners of Jewell county. The firm is reliable. See White Rock advertisements.

CHURCHES.

M. E., Rev. Wright, Pastor. Baptist, Rev. Howard, Pastor. Presbyterian, Rev. J. F. Donaldson, Pastor.

The Odd Fellows have a flourishing Lodge.

There is a fine stone school house with regular terms of school.

The town of White Rock was located in 1871. The Town Company consisted of the following named persons: S. R. Morlan, Thos. Lovewell, A. B. Ogle, Ed. Laney, Chester Babcock and G. W. Reynolds.

THE FUTURE.

The Central Branch U. P. Railroad has a line surveyed through the southern part of Jewell county, passing close to Jewell City. This road will be built during the summer of 1878. A branch of the Kansas Pacific will be built this year from Solomon City to Beloit, 15 miles south of Jewell City. It is generally believed this road will be extended at an early day from Beloit through Jewell county, touching the towns of Jewell City, Jewell Centre, Burr Oak and Salem, and connecting with a branch of the Burlington and Missouri railroad at Red Cloud, Neb. This will insure the grandest developement of a county that has, without a road, outstripped almost every other county in the State.

PRESENT OFFICERS OF JEWELL COUNTY.

		Address:	
Board of Com's'r's.	B. F. Ransford, Ch'r'n.		Jewell City.
	Thos. Shuler,	"	White Rock.
	O. F. Roberts,	"	Burr Oak.
Present Treasurer	John Burns,	"	Jewell Centre.
Treasurer elect	W. C. McClung,	"	Jewell City.
County Clerk	Wm. M. Allen,	"	Jewell Centre.
Sheriff	John Shives,	"	" "
Probate Judge	J. W. McRoberts,	"	" "
Register of Deeds	Manoah Stone,	"	" "
Sup't. Pub. Inst.	D. S. Kenney,	"	" "
County Surveyor	E. T. Byram,	"	Jewell City.
" Coroner	Dr. Walter Crew,	"	Jewell Centre.
Clerk of the Dis't. Court,	D. J. Vance,	"	" "
County Attorney	C. Angevine,	"	" "

Representatives from Jewell County.

		Address:	
108th Dist.	G. S. Bishop,		Jewell Centre.
109th "	D. L. Palmer,	"	Jewell City.

State Senator.

		Address:	
34th Senat'l Dist.	T. B. Carpenter,		Burr Oak.

Judge of the 15th Judicial District.

		Address:	
Joel Holt.			Beloit, Kansas.

www.ingramcontent.com/pod-product-compliance
Lightning Source LLC
Chambersburg PA
CBHW021439090426
42739CB00009B/1556